PRACTICE THE PERT WITH THIS BOOK

Postsecondary Education Readiness Test Practice Questions

Copyright © 2017 by Complete Test Preparation Inc. ALL RIGHTS RESERVED. No part of this book may be reproduced or transferred in any form or by any means, graphic, electronic, or mechanical, including photocopying, recording, web distribution, taping, or by any information storage retrieval system, without the written permission of the author.

Notice: Complete Test Preparation Inc. makes every reasonable effort to obtain from reliable sources accurate, complete, and timely information about the tests covered in this book. Nevertheless, changes can be made in the tests or the administration of the tests at any time and Complete Test Preparation Inc. makes no representation or warranty, either expressed or implied as to the accuracy, timeliness, or completeness of the information contained in this book. Complete Test Preparation Inc. makes no representations or warranties of any kind, express or implied, about the completeness, accuracy, reliability, suitability or availability with respect to the information contained in this document for any purpose. Any reliance you place on such information is therefore strictly at your own risk.

The author(s) shall not be liable for any loss incurred as a consequence of the use and application, directly or indirectly, of any information presented in this work. Sold with the understanding, the author(s) is not engaged in rendering professional services or advice. If advice or expert assistance is required, the services of a competent professional should be sought.

The company, product and service names used in this publication are for identification purposes only. All trademarks and registered trademarks are the property of their respective owners. Complete Test Preparation Inc. is not affiliated with any educational institution.

The PERT Exam is administered by the Florida Department of Education, who are not involved in the production of, and do not endorse this publication.

We strongly recommend that students check with exam providers for up-to-date information regarding test content.

ISBN-13: 9781772452686

Version 7.5 May 2018

About Complete Test Preparation Inc.

The Complete Test Preparation Team has been publishing high quality study materials since 2005. Over 1 million students visit our websites every year, and thousands of students, teachers and parents all over the world (over 100 countries) have purchased our teaching materials, curriculum, study guides and practice tests.

Complete Test Preparation is committed to providing students with the best study materials and practice tests available on the market. Members of our team combine years of teaching experience, with experienced writers and editors, all with advanced degrees.

Feedback

Find us on Facebook

www.facebook.com/CompleteTestPreparation

CONTENTS

6   **Getting Started**
       The PERT Study Plan   7
       Making a Study Schedule   8

14   **Practice Test Questions Set 1**
       Answer Key   53

72   **Practice Test Questions Set 2**
       Answer Key   109

Getting Started

CONGRATULATIONS! By deciding to take the Florida Post Secondary Readiness Test (PERT), you have taken the first step toward a great future! Of course, there is no point in taking this important examination unless you intend to do your best to earn the highest grade you possibly can. That means getting yourself organized and discovering the best approaches, methods and strategies to master the material. Yes, that will require real effort and dedication on your part but if you are willing to focus your energy and devote the study time necessary, before you know it you will be on you will be opening that letter of acceptance to the school of your dreams!

We know that taking on a new endeavour can be a little scary, and it is easy to feel unsure of where to begin. That's where we come in. This study guide is designed to help you improve your test-taking skills, show you a few tricks of the trade and increase both your competency and confidence.

The PERT Exam

The PERT exam is composed of three main sections, reading, mathematics, and writing. The reading section consists of reading comprehension, analysis of written passages and meaning in context. The mathematics section contains, arithmetic, algebra, geometry and polynomials and quadratic equations. The writing skills section contains questions on sentence structure and rewriting sentences. The writing section contains an essay question, as well as English grammar, spelling, punctuation and usage.

The PERT exam is computer based and adaptive. This means if you answer a questions correctly, the next question will be more difficulty until you reach your level of difficulty. If you answer incorrectly and you are not already at the lowest level of difficulty, the next question will be easier. Each question is multiple-choice, and the exact number of questions varies from student to student depending on how skilled the student is in a particular area.

While we seek to make our guide as comprehensive as possible, note that like all exams, the PERT Exam might be adjusted at some future point. New material might be added, or content that is no longer relevant or applicable might be removed. It is always a good idea to give the materials you receive when you register a careful review.

THE PERT STUDY PLAN

Now that you have made the decision to take the PERT, it is time to get started. Before you do another thing, you will need to figure out a plan of attack. The very best study tip is to start early! The longer the time period you devote to regular study practice, the more likely you will be to retain the material and be able to access it quickly. If you thought that 1x20 is the same as 2x10, guess what? It really is not, when it comes to study time. Reviewing material for just an hour per day over the course of 20 days is far better than studying for two hours a day for only 10 days. The more often you revisit a particular piece of information, the better you will know it. Not only will your grasp and understanding be better, but your ability to reach into your brain and quickly and efficiently pull out the tidbit you need, will be greatly enhanced as well.

The great Chinese scholar and philosopher Confucius believed that true knowledge could be defined as knowing both what you know and what you do not know. The first step in preparing for the PERT is to assess your strengths and weaknesses. You may already have an idea of what you know and what you do not know, but evaluating yourself using our Self- Assessment modules for each of the three areas, Math, Writing and Reading Comprehension, will clarify the details.

Making a Study Schedule

To make your study time most productive you will need to develop a study plan. The purpose of the plan is to organize all the bits of pieces of information in such a way that you will not feel overwhelmed. Rome was not built in a day, and learning everything you will need to know to pass the PERT is going to take time, too. Arranging the material you need to learn into manageable chunks is the best way to go. Each study session should make you feel as though you have succeeded in accomplishing your goal, and your goal is simply to learn what you planned to learn during that particular session. Try to organize the content in such a way that each study session builds on previous ones. That way, you will retain the information, be better able to access it, and review the previous bits and pieces at the same time.

Self-assessment

The Best Study Tip! The very best study tip is to start early! The longer you study regularly, the more you will retain and 'learn' the material. Studying for 1 hour per day for 20 days is far better than studying for 2 hours for 10 days.

What don't you know?

The first step is to assess your strengths and weaknesses. You may already have an idea of where your weaknesses are, or you can take our Self-assessment modules for each of the areas, Reading Comprehension, Arithmetic, Essay Writing, Algebra and College Level Math.

Exam Component	Rate 1 to 5
Reading Comprehension	
Making Inferences	
Main idea	
Arithmetic	
Decimals Percent and Fractions	
Problem solving (Word Problems)	
Basic Algebra	
Simple Geometry	
Problem Solving	
Essay and English	
Essay Writing	
Basic English Grammar and Usage	
Spelling	
Punctuation	
Capitalization	
Mathematics	
Linear Equations	
Quadratics	
Polynomials	
Coordinate Geometry	

Making a Study Schedule

The key to making a study plan is to divide the material you need to learn into manageable size and learn it, while at the same time reviewing the material that you already know.

Using the table above, any scores of three or below, you need to spend time learning, going over, and practicing this subject area. A score of four means you need to review the material, but you don't have to spend time re-learning. A score of five and you are OK with just an occasional review before the exam.

A score of zero or one means you really do need to work on this and you should allocate the most time and give it the highest priority. Some students prefer a 5-day plan and others a 10-day plan. It also depends on how much time you have until the exam.

Here is an example of a 5-day plan based on an example from the table above:

Main Idea: 1   Study 1 hour everyday – review on last day
Linear Equations: 3   Study 1 hour for 2 days then ½ hour and then review
Algebra: 4   Review every second day
Grammar & Usage: 2 Study 1 hour on the first day – then ½ hour everyday
Reading Comprehension: 5   Review for ½ hour every other day
Geometry: 5 Review for ½ hour every other day

Using this example, geometry and reading comprehension are good and only need occasional review. Algebra is good and needs 'some' review. Linear Equations need a bit of work, grammar and usage needs a lot of work and Main Idea is very weak and need most of time. Based on this, here is a sample study plan:

Day	Subject	Time
Monday		
Study	Main Idea	1 hour
Study	Grammar & Usage	1 hour
	½ hour break	
Study	Linear Equations	1 hour
Review	Algebra	½ hour
Tuesday		
Study	Main Idea	1 hour
Study	Grammar & Usage	½ hour
	½ hour break	
Study	Linear Equations	½ hour
Review	Algebra	½ hour
Review	Geometry	½ hour
Wednesday		
Study	Main Idea	1 hour
Study	Grammar & Usage	½ hour
	½ hour break	
Study	Linear Equations	½ hour
Review	Geometry	½ hour
Thursday		
Study	Main Idea	½ hour
Study	Grammar & Usage	½ hour
Review	Linear Equations	½ hour
	½ hour break	
Review	Geometry	½ hour
Review	Algebra	½ hour
Friday		
Review	Main Idea	½ hour
Review	Grammar & Usage	½ hour
Review	Linear Equations	½ hour
	½ hour break	
Review	Algebra	½ hour
Review	Grammar & Usage	½ hour

Using this example, adapt the study plan to your own schedule. This schedule assumes 2 ½ - 3 hours available to study everyday for a 5 day period.

First, write out what you need to study and how much. Next figure out how many days you have before the test. Note, do NOT study on the last day before the test. On the last day before the test, you won't learn anything and will probably only confuse yourself.

Make a table with the days before the test and the number of hours you have available to study each day. We suggest working with 1 hour and ½ hour time slots.

Start filling in the blanks, with the subjects you need to study the most getting the most time and the most regular time slots (i.e. everyday) and the subjects that you know getting the least time (e.g. ½ hour every other day, or every 3rd day).

Tips for making a schedule

Once you make a schedule, stick with it! Make your study sessions reasonable. If you make a study schedule and don't stick with it, you set yourself up for failure. Instead, schedule study sessions that are a bit shorter and set yourself up for success! Make sure your study sessions are do-able. Studying is hard work but after you pass, you can party and take a break!

Schedule breaks. Breaks are just as important as study time. Work out a rotation of studying and breaks that works for you.

Build up study time. If you find it hard to sit still and study for 1 hour straight through, build up to it. Start with 20 minutes, and then take a break. Once you get used to 20-minute study sessions, increase the time to 30 minutes. Gradually work you way up to 1 hour.

40 minutes to 1 hour are optimal. Studying for longer than this is tiring and not productive. Studying for shorter isn't long enough to be productive.

Studying Math. Studying Math is different from studying other subjects because you use a different part of your brain. The best way to study math is to practice everyday. This will train your mind to think in a mathematical way. If you miss a day or days, the mathematical mind-set is gone and you have to start all over again to build it up.

Study and practice math everyday for at least 5 days before the exam.

PRACTICE TEST QUESTIONS SET 1

The questions below are not the same as you will find on the PERT - that would be too easy! And nobody knows what the questions will be and they change all the time. Below are general questions that cover the same subject areas as the PERT. So, while the format and exact wording of the questions may differ slightly, and change from year to year, if you can answer the questions below, you will have no problem with the PERT.

For the best results, take these practice test questions as if it were the real exam. Set aside time when you will not be disturbed, and a location that is quiet and free of distractions. Read the instructions carefully, read each question carefully, and answer to the best of your ability.
Use the bubble answer sheets provided. When you have completed the practice questions, check your answer against the Answer Key and read the explanation provided.

Do not attempt more than one set of practice test questions in one day. After completing the first practice test, wait two or three days before attempting the second set of questions.

Reading Answer Sheet

	A	B	C	D	E			A	B	C	D	E
1	○	○	○	○	○		21	○	○	○	○	○
2	○	○	○	○	○		22	○	○	○	○	○
3	○	○	○	○	○		23	○	○	○	○	○
4	○	○	○	○	○		24	○	○	○	○	○
5	○	○	○	○	○		25	○	○	○	○	○
6	○	○	○	○	○		26	○	○	○	○	○
7	○	○	○	○	○		27	○	○	○	○	○
8	○	○	○	○	○		28	○	○	○	○	○
9	○	○	○	○	○		29	○	○	○	○	○
10	○	○	○	○	○		30	○	○	○	○	○
11	○	○	○	○	○							
12	○	○	○	○	○							
13	○	○	○	○	○							
14	○	○	○	○	○							
15	○	○	○	○	○							
16	○	○	○	○	○							
17	○	○	○	○	○							
18	○	○	○	○	○							
19	○	○	○	○	○							
20	○	○	○	○	○							

Mathematics Answer Sheet

	A	B	C	D	E			A	B	C	D	E
1	○	○	○	○	○		21	○	○	○	○	○
2	○	○	○	○	○		22	○	○	○	○	○
3	○	○	○	○	○		23	○	○	○	○	○
4	○	○	○	○	○		24	○	○	○	○	○
5	○	○	○	○	○		25	○	○	○	○	○
6	○	○	○	○	○		26	○	○	○	○	○
7	○	○	○	○	○		27	○	○	○	○	○
8	○	○	○	○	○		28	○	○	○	○	○
9	○	○	○	○	○		29	○	○	○	○	○
10	○	○	○	○	○		30	○	○	○	○	○
11	○	○	○	○	○							
12	○	○	○	○	○							
13	○	○	○	○	○							
14	○	○	○	○	○							
15	○	○	○	○	○							
16	○	○	○	○	○							
17	○	○	○	○	○							
18	○	○	○	○	○							
19	○	○	○	○	○							
20	○	○	○	○	○							

Writing Skills Answer Sheet

	A	B	C	D	E			A	B	C	D	E
1	○	○	○	○	○		21	○	○	○	○	○
2	○	○	○	○	○		22	○	○	○	○	○
3	○	○	○	○	○		23	○	○	○	○	○
4	○	○	○	○	○		24	○	○	○	○	○
5	○	○	○	○	○		25	○	○	○	○	○
6	○	○	○	○	○		26	○	○	○	○	○
7	○	○	○	○	○		27	○	○	○	○	○
8	○	○	○	○	○		28	○	○	○	○	○
9	○	○	○	○	○		29	○	○	○	○	○
10	○	○	○	○	○		30	○	○	○	○	○
11	○	○	○	○	○							
12	○	○	○	○	○							
13	○	○	○	○	○							
14	○	○	○	○	○							
15	○	○	○	○	○							
16	○	○	○	○	○							
17	○	○	○	○	○							
18	○	○	○	○	○							
19	○	○	○	○	○							
20	○	○	○	○	○							

Reading and Language Arts

Directions: The following questions are based on several reading passages. A series of questions follow each passage. Read each passage carefully, and then answer the questions based on it. You may reread the passage as often as you wish. When you have finished answering the questions based on one passage, go right onto the next passage. Choose the best answer based on the information given and implied.

Questions 1 – 4 refer to the following passage.

Passage 1 - The Life of Helen Keller

Many people have heard of Helen Keller. She is famous because she was unable to see or hear, but learned to speak and read and went onto attend college and earn a degree. Her life is a very interesting story, one that she developed into an autobiography, which was then adapted into both a stage play and a movie. How did Helen Keller overcome her disabilities to become a famous woman? Read onto find out. Helen Keller was not born blind and deaf. When she was a small baby, she had a very high fever for several days. As a result of her sudden illness, baby Helen lost her eyesight and her hearing. Because she was so young when she went deaf and blind, Helen Keller never had any recollection of being able to see or hear. Since she could not hear, she could not learn to talk. Since she could not see, it was difficult for her to move around. For the first six years of her life, her world was very still and dark.

Imagine what Helen's childhood was like. She could not hear her mother's voice. She could not see the beauty of her parent's farm. She could not recognize who was giving her a hug, or a bath or even where her bedroom was each night. More sad, she could not communicate with her parents in any way. She could not express her feelings or tell them the things she wanted. It must have been a very sad childhood.

When Helen was six years old, her parents hired her a

teacher named Anne Sullivan. Anne was a young woman who was almost blind. However, she could hear and she could read Braille, so she was a perfect teacher for young Helen. At first, Anne had a very hard time teaching Helen anything. She described her first impression of Helen as a "wild thing, not a child." Helen did not like Anne at first either. She bit and hit Anne when Anne tried to teach her. However, the two of them eventually came to have a great deal of love and respect.

Anne taught Helen to hear by putting her hands on people's throats. She could feel the sounds that people made. In time, Helen learned to feel what people said. Next, Anne taught Helen to read Braille, which is a way that books are written for the blind. Finally, Anne taught Helen to talk. Although Helen did learn to talk, it was hard for anyone but Anne to understand her.

As Helen grew older, more and more people were amazed by her story. She went to college and wrote books about her life. She gave talks to the public, with Anne at her side, translating her words. Today, both Anne Sullivan and Helen Keller are famous women who are respected for their lives' work.

1. Helen Keller could not see and hear and so, what was her biggest problem in childhood?

    a. Inability to communicate

    b. Inability to walk

    c. Inability to play

    d. Inability to eat

2. Helen learned to hear by feeling the vibrations people made when they spoke. What were these vibrations were felt through?

    a. Mouth

    b. Throat

    c. Ears

    d. Lips

3. From the passage, we can infer that Anne Sullivan was a patient teacher. We can infer this because

    a. Helen hit and bit her and Anne still remained her teacher.

    b. Anne taught Helen to read only.

    c. Anne was hard of hearing too.

    d. Anne wanted to be a teacher.

4. Helen Keller learned to speak but Anne translated her words when she spoke in public. The reason Helen needed a translator was because

    a. Helen spoke another language.

    b. Helen's words were hard for people to understand.

    c. Helen spoke very quietly.

    d. Helen did not speak but only used sign language.

Questions 5 – 7 refer to the following passage.

Passage 2 - Ways Characters Communicate in Theater

Playwrights give their characters voices in a way that gives depth and added meaning to what happens on stage during their play. There are different types of speech in scripts that allow characters to talk with themselves, with other characters, and even with the audience.

It is very unique to theater that characters may talk "to themselves." When characters do this, the speech they give is called a soliloquy. Soliloquies are usually poetic, introspective, moving, and can tell audience members about the feelings, motivations, or suspicions of an individual character without that character having to reveal them to other characters on stage. "To be or not to be" is a famous soliloquy given by Hamlet as he considers difficult but important themes, such as life and death.

The most common type of communication in plays is when one character is speaking to another or a group of other characters. This is generally called dialogue, but can also be called monologue if one character speaks without being interrupted for a long time. It is not necessarily the most important type of communication, but it is the most common because the plot of the play cannot really progress without it.

Lastly, and most unique to theater (although it has been used somewhat in film) is when a character speaks directly to the audience. This is called an aside, and scripts usually specifically direct actors to do this. Asides are usually comical, an inside joke between the character and the audience, and very short. The actor will usually face the audience when delivering them, even if it's for a moment, so the audience can recognize this move as an aside.

All three of these types of communication are important to the art of theater, and have been perfected by famous playwrights like Shakespeare. Understanding these types of communication can help an audience member grasp what is artful about the script and action of a play.

5. According to the passage, characters in plays communicate to

    a. move the plot forward

    b. show the private thoughts and feelings of one character

    c. make the audience laugh

    d. add beauty and artistry to the play

6. When Hamlet delivers "To be or not to be," he can most likely be described as

    a. solitary

    b. thoughtful

    c. dramatic

    d. hopeless

7. The author uses parentheses to punctuate "although it has been used somewhat in film,"

    a. to show that films are less important

    b. instead of using commas so that the sentence is not interrupted

    c. because parenthesis help separate details that are not as important

    d. to show that films are not as artistic

Questions 8 – 10 refer to the following passage.

Passage 3 - Low Blood Sugar

As the name suggest, low blood sugar is low sugar levels in the bloodstream. This can occur when you have not eaten properly and undertake strenuous activity, or, when you are very hungry. When Low blood sugar occurs regularly and is ongoing, it is a medical condition called hypoglycemia. This condition can occur in diabetics and in healthy adults.

Causes of low blood sugar can include excessive alcohol consumption, metabolic problems, stomach surgery, pancreas, liver or kidneys problems, as well as a side-effect of some medications.

Symptoms

There are different symptoms depending on the severity of the case.

Mild hypoglycemia can lead to feelings of nausea and hunger. The patient may also feel nervous, jittery and have fast heart beats. Sweaty skin, clammy and cold skin are likely symptoms.
Moderate hypoglycemia can result in a short temper, confusion, nervousness, fear and blurring of vision. The patient may feel weak and unsteady.

Severe cases of hypoglycemia can lead to seizures, coma,

fainting spells, nightmares, headaches, excessive sweats and severe tiredness.

Diagnosis of low blood sugar

A doctor can diagnosis this medical condition by asking the patient questions and testing blood and urine samples. Home testing kits are available for patients to monitor blood sugar levels. It is important to see a qualified doctor though. The doctor can administer tests to ensure that will safely rule out other medical conditions that could affect blood sugar levels.

Treatment

Quick treatments include drinking or eating foods and drinks with high sugar contents. Good examples include soda, fruit juice, hard candy and raisins. Glucose energy tablets can also help. Doctors may also recommend medications and well as changes in diet and exercise routine to treat chronic low blood sugar.

8. Based on the article, which of the following is true?

    a. Low blood sugar can happen to anyone.

    b. Low blood sugar only happens to diabetics.

    c. Low blood sugar can occur even.

    d. None of the statements are true.

9. Which of the following are the author's opinion?

    a. Quick treatments include drinking or eating foods and drinks with high sugar contents.

    b. None of the statements are opinions.

    c. This condition can occur in diabetics and also in healthy adults.

    d. There are different symptoms depending on the severity of the case

10. What is the author's purpose?

    a. To inform

    b. To persuade

    c. To entertain

    d. To analyze

11. Which of the following is not a detail?

    a. A doctor can diagnosis this medical condition by asking the patient questions and testing.

    b. A doctor will test blood and urine samples.

    c. Glucose energy tablets can also help.

    d. Home test kits monitor blood sugar levels.

    d. None of the above.

Questions 12 – 15 refer to the following passage.

How To Get A Good Nights Sleep

Sleep is just as essential for healthy living as water, air and food. Sleep allows the body to rest and replenish depleted energy levels. Sometimes we may for various reasons experience difficulty sleeping which has a serious effect on our health. Those who have prolonged sleeping problems are facing a serious medical condition and should see a qualified doctor when possible for help. Here is simple guide that can help you sleep better at night.

Try to create a natural pattern of waking up and sleeping around the same time everyday. This means avoiding going to bed too early and oversleeping past your usual wake up time. Going to bed and getting up at radically different times everyday confuses your body clock. Try to establish a natural rhythm as much as you can.

Exercises and a bit of physical activity can help you sleep better at night. If you are having problem sleeping, try to be as active as you can during the day. If you are tired from physical activity, falling asleep is a natural and easy process for your body. If you remain inactive during the day, you will find it harder to sleep properly at night. Try walking, jogging, swimming or simple stretches as you get close to your bed time.

Afternoon naps are great to refresh you during the day, but they may also keep you awake at night. If you feel sleepy during the day, get up, take a walk and get busy to keep from sleeping. Stretching is a good way to increase blood flow to the brain and keep you alert so that you don't sleep during the day. This will help you sleep better night.

> A warm bath or a glass of milk in the evening can help your body relax and prepare for sleep. A cold bath will wake you up and keep you up for several hours. Also avoid eating too late before bed.

12. How would you describe this sentence?

    a. A recommendation

    b. An opinion

    c. A fact

    d. A diagnosis

13. Which of the following is an alternative title for this article?

    a. Exercise and a good night's sleep

    b. Benefits of a good night's sleep

    c. Tips for a good night's sleep

    d. Lack of sleep is a serious medical condition

14. Which of the following cannot be inferred from this article?

a. Biking is helpful for getting a good night's sleep

b. Mental activity is helpful for getting a good night's sleep

c. Eating bedtime snacks is not recommended

d. Getting up at the same time is helpful for a good night's sleep

15. What is a disadvantage of taking naps?

a. They may keep you awake.

b. There are no disadvantages

c. They may help you sleep better

d. They may affect your diet

Question 16 refers to the following Table of Contents.

Contents

    Science Self-assessment 81
    Answer Key 91
    Science Tutorials 96
    Scientific Method 96
    Biology 99
    Heredity: Genes and Mutation 104
    Classification 108
    Ecology 110
    Chemistry 112
    Energy: Kinetic and Mechanical 126
    Energy: Work and Power 130
    Force: Newton's Three Laws 132

16. Consider the table of contents above. What page would you find information about natural selection and adaptation?

    a. 81
    b. 90
    c. 110
    d. 132

Questions 17 – 19 refer to the following passage.

Passage 5 - Pearl Harbor

A Day That Will Live in Infamy! Attack on Pearl Harbor
In 1941, the world was at war. The United States was trying very hard to keep itself out of the conflict. In Europe, the countries of Germany and Italy had formed an alliance to expand their land and territory. Germany had already taken over Poland, Denmark, and parts of France. They were heading next toward England and due to all the fighting in Europe, there were battles taking place as far south as North Africa, where the German and Italian armies were fighting the British.

This got even worse when the Asian nation of Japan formed an alliance with Germany and Italy. Together, the three countries called themselves, the AXIS. Now, the war was in the Pacific as well as in Europe and Northern Africa. A great deal of Americans felt that perhaps now was the time for the United States to join with its ally, Great Britain and stop the Axis from taking over more regions of the world.

In 1941, Franklin Roosevelt was President of the United States. His fear at the time was that Japan would try to take over many countries in Asia. He did not want to see that happen, so he moved some of the United States warships that had been stationed in San Diego, to the military base at Pearl Harbor, in Honolulu, Hawaii.

Japan quietly plotted their attack. They waited until the early hours of the morning on Sunday, December 7, 1941.

Then, 350 Japanese war plans began to drop bombs on the U.S. ships at Pearl Harbor. The first bombs fell at 7:48 am and a mere 90 minutes later, the attack was over. Pearl Harbor was decimated. 8 battleships were damaged. Eleven ships were sunk and 300 U.S. planes were destroyed. Most devastating was the loss of life 2,400 U.S. military members was killed in the attack and 1, 282 were injured.

President Roosevelt addressed the country via the radio and said "Today is a day that will live in infamy." He asked Congress to declare war on Japan. War was declared on Japan on December 8th and on Germany and Italy on December 11th. The United States had entered World War Two.

17. After reading the passage, what can we infer infamy means?

    a. Famous

    b. Remembered in a good way

    c. Remembered in a bad way

    d. Easily forgotten

18. What three countries formed the Axis?

    a. Italy, England, Germany

    b. United States, England, Italy

    c. Germany, Japan, Italy

    d. Germany, Japan, United States

19. What do you think was President Roosevelt's reason for moving warships to Pearl Harbor?

    a. He feared Japan would bomb San Diego

    b. He knew Japan was going to attack Pearl Harbor

    c. He was planning to attack Japan

    d. He wanted to try and protect Asian countries from Japanese takeover

20. Why do you think Japan chose a Sunday morning at 7:48 am for their attack?

a. They knew the military slept late

b. There is a law against bombing countries on a Sunday

c. They wanted the attack to catch people by surprise

d. That was the only free time they had to attack.

Questions 21 - 24 refer to the following recipe.

If You Have Allergies, You're Not Alone

People who experience allergies might joke that their immune systems have let them down or are seriously lacking. Truthfully though, people who experience allergic reactions or allergy symptoms during certain times of the year have heightened immune systems that are, "better" than those of people who have perfectly healthy but less militant immune systems.

Still, when a person has an allergic reaction, they are having an adverse reaction to a substance that is considered normal to most people. Mild allergic reactions usually have symptoms like itching, runny nose, red eyes, or bumps or discoloration of the skin. More serious allergic reactions, such as those to animal and insect poisons or certain foods, may result in the closing of the throat, swelling of the eyes, low blood pressure, inability to breath, and can even be fatal.

Different treatments help different allergies, and which one a person uses depends on the nature and severity of the allergy. It is recommended to patients with severe allergies to take extra precautions, such as carrying an EpiPen, which treats anaphylactic shock and may prevent death, always in order for the remedy to be readily available and more effective. When an allergy is not so severe, treatments may be used just relieve a person of uncomfortable symptoms. Over the counter allergy medicines treat milder symptoms, and can be bought at any grocery store and used in moderation to help people with allergies live normally.

There are many tests available to assess whether a person has allergies or what they may be allergic to, and advances in these tests and the medicine used to treat patients continues to improve. Despite this fact, allergies still affect many people throughout the year or even every day. Medicines used to treat allergies have side effects of their own, and it is difficult to bring the body into balance with the use of medicine. Regardless, many of those who live with allergies are grateful for what is available and find it useful in maintaining their lifestyles.

21. According to this passage, it can be understood that the word "militant" belongs in a group with the words:

    a. sickly, ailing, faint

    b. strength, power, vigor

    c. active, fighting, warring

    d. worn, tired, breaking down

22. The author says that "medicines used to treat allergies have side-effects of their own" to

    a. point out that doctors aren't very good at diagnosing and treating allergies

    b. argue that because of the large number of people with allergies, a cure will never be found

    c. explain that allergy medicines aren't cures and some compromise must be made

    d. argue that more wholesome remedies should be researched and medicines banned

23. It can be inferred that _____ recommend that some people with allergies carry medicine with them.

    a. the author

    b. doctors

    c. the makers of EpiPen

    d. people with allergies

24. The author has written this passage to

   a. inform readers on symptoms of allergies so people with allergies can get help

   b. persuade readers to be proud of having allergies

   c. inform readers on different remedies so people with allergies receive the right help

   d. describe different types of allergies, their symptoms, and their remedies

Questions 25 – 26 refer to the following email.

SUBJECT: MEDICAL STAFF CHANGES

To all staff:

This email is to advise you of a paper on recommended medical staff changes has been posted to the Human Resources website.

The contents are of primary interest to medical staff, other staff may be interested in reading it, particularly those in medical support roles.

The paper deals with several major issues:

   1. Improving our ability to attract top quality staff to the hospital, and retain our existing staff. These changes will make our position and departmental names internationally recognizable and comparable with North American and North Asian departments and positions.

   2. Improving our ability to attract top quality staff by introducing greater flexibility in the departmental structure.

   3. General comments on issues to be further discussed in relation to research staff.

The changes outlined in this paper are significant. I encourage you to read the document and send to me any comments you may have, so that it can be enhanced and improved.

Gordon Simms
Administrator,
Seven Oaks Regional Hospital

25. Are all hospital staff required to read the document posted to the Human Resources website?

    a. Yes all staff are required to read the document.

    b. No, reading the document is optional.

    c. Only medical staff are required to read the document.

    d. none of the above are correct.

26. Have the changes to medical staff been made?

    a. Yes, the changes have been made.

    b. No, the changes are only being discussed.

    c. Some of the changes have been made.

    d. None of the choices are correct.

Questions 27 – 30 refer to the following passage.

When a Poet Longs to Mourn, He Writes an Elegy

Poems are an expressive, especially emotional, form of writing. They have been present in literature virtually from the time civilizations invented the written word. Poets often portrayed as moody, secluded, and even troubled, but this is because poets are introspective and feel deeply about the current events and cultural norms they are surrounded with. Poets often produce the most telling literature, giving insight into the society and mind-set they come from. This can be done in many forms.

The oldest types of poems often include many stanzas, may or may not rhyme, and are more about telling a story than experimenting with language or words. The most common types of ancient poetry are epics, which are usually extremely long stories that follow a hero through his journey, or ellegies, which are often solemn in tone and used to mourn or lament something or someone. The Mesopotamians are often said to have invented the written word, and their literature is among the oldest in the world, including the epic poem titled "Epic of Gilgamesh." Similar in style and length to "Gilgamesh" is "Beowulf," an ellegy written in Old English and set in Scandinavia. These poems are often used by professors as the earliest examples of literature.

The importance of poetry was revived in the Renaissance. At this time, Europeans discovered the style and beauty of ancient Greek arts, and poetry was among those. Shakespeare is the most well-known poet of the time, and he used poetry not only to write poems but also to write plays for the theater. The most popular forms of poetry during the Renaissance included villanelles, (a nineteen-line poetic form) sonnets, as well as the epic. Poets during this time focused on style and form, and developed very specific rules and outlines for how an exceptional poem should be written.

As often happens in the arts, modern poets have rejected the constricting rules of Renaissance poets, and free form poems are much more popular. Some modern poems would read just like stories if they weren't arranged into lines and stanzas. It is difficult to tell which poems and poets will be the most important, because works of art often become more famous in hindsight, after the poet has died and society can look at itself without being in the moment. Modern poetry continues to develop, and will no doubt continue to change as values, thought, and writing continue to change.

Poems can be among the most enlightening and uplifting texts for a person to read if they are looking to connect with the past, connect with other people, or try to gain an understanding of what is happening in their time.

27. In summary, the author has written this passage

   a. as a foreword that will introduce a poem in a book or magazine

   b. because she loves poetry and wants more people to like it

   c. to give a brief history of poems

   d. to convince students to write poems

28. The author organizes the paragraphs mainly by

   a. moving chronologically, explaining which types of poetry were common in that time

   b. talking about new types of poems each paragraph and explaining them a little

   c. focusing on one poet or group of people and the poems they wrote

   d. explaining older types of poetry so she can talk about modern poetry

29. The author's claim that poetry has been around "virtually from the time civilizations invented the written word" is supported by the detail that

   a. Beowulf is written in Old English, which is not really in use any longer

   b. epic poems told stories about heroes

   c. the Renaissance poets tried to copy Greek poets

   d. the Mesopotamians are credited with both inventing the word and writing "Epic of Gilgamesh"

30. According to the passage, it can be understood that the word "telling" means

   a. speaking

   b. significant

   c. soothing

   d. wordy

MATHEMATICS

1. Divide 243 by 3^3

    a. 243
    b. 11
    c. 9
    d. 27

2. Solve the following equation 4(y + 6) = 3y + 30

    a. y = 20
    b. y = 6
    c. y = 30/7
    d. y = 30

3. Divide $x^2 - y^2$ by x - y.

    a. x - y
    b. x + y
    c. xy
    d. y - x

4. Solve for x if, $10^2 \times 100^2 = 1000^x$

    a. x = 2
    b. x = 3
    c. x = -2
    d. x = 0

5. Given polynomials A = -2x⁴ + x² - 3x, B = x⁴ - x³ + 5 and C = x⁴ + 2x³ + 4x + 5, find A + B - C.

   a. $x^3 + x^2 + x + 10$
   b. $-3x^3 + x^2 - 7x + 10$
   c. $-2x^4 - 3x^3 + x^2 - 7x$
   d. $-3x^4 + x^3 + 2 - 7x$

6. Solve the inequality: $(x - 6)^2 \geq x^2 + 12$

   a. $(2, +\infty)$
   b. $(2, +\infty)$
   c. $(-\infty, 2]$
   d. $(12, +\infty)$

7. $7^5 - 3^5 =$

   a. 15,000
   b. 16,564
   c. 15,800
   d. 15,007

8. Divide $x^3 - 3x^2 + 3x - 1$ by $x - 1$.

   a. $x^2 - 1$
   b. $x^2 + 1$
   c. $x^2 - 2x + 1$
   d. $x^2 + 2x + 1$

9. Express 9 x 9 x 9 in exponential form and standard form.

   a. $9^3 = 719$
   b. $9^3 = 629$
   c. $9^3 = 729$
   d. $10^3 = 729$

10. Using the factoring method, solve the quadratic equation: $x^2 - 5x - 6 = 0$

    a. -6 and 1
    b. -1 and 6
    c. 1 and 6
    d. -6 and -1

11. Divide 0.524 by 10^3

    a. 0.0524
    b. 0.000524
    c. 0.00524
    d. 524

12. Factor the polynomial $x^3y^3 - x^2y^8$.

    a. $x^2y^3(x - y^5)$
    b. $x^3y^3(1 - y^5)$
    c. $x^2y^2(x - y^6)$
    d. $xy^3(x - y^5)$

13. Find the solution for the following linear equation: $5x/2 = 3x + 24/6$

    a. -1
    b. 0
    c. 1
    d. 2

14. $3^2 \times 3^5$

    a. 3^{17}
    b. 3^5
    c. 4^8
    d. 3^7

15. Solve the system, if a is some real number:

$ax + y = 1$
$x + ay = 1$

    a. (1,a)
    b. (1/a + 1, 1)
    c. (1/(a + 1), 1/(a + 1))
    d. (a, 1/a + 1)

16. Solve $3^5 \div 3^8$

    a. 3^3
    b. 3^5
    c. 3^6
    d. 3^4

17. Solve the linear equation: $3(x + 2) - 2(1 - x) = 4x + 5$

    a. -1
    b. 0
    c. 1
    d. 2

18. Simplify the following expression: $3x^a + 6a^x - x^a + (-5a^x) - 2x^a$

    a. $a^x + x^a$
    b. $a^x - x^a$
    c. a^x
    d. x^a

19. Add polynomials $-3x^2 + 2x + 6$ and $-x^2 - x - 1$.

a. $-2x^2 + x + 5$
b. $-4x^2 + x + 5$
c. $-2x^2 + 3x + 5$
d. $-4x^2 + 3x + 5$

20. 10^4 is not equal to which of the following?

a. 100,000
b. 10 x 10 x 10 x 10
c. 10^2 x 10^2
d. 10,000

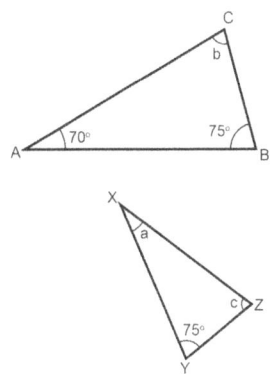

21. What are the respective values of a, b & c if both triangles are similar?

a. 70°, 70°, 35°
b. 70°, 35°, 70°
c. 35°, 35°, 35°
d. 70°, 35°, 35°

22. Consider 2 triangles, ABC and A'B'C', where:

BC = B' C'
AC = A' C'
RA = RA'

Are these 2 triangles congruent?

a. Yes
b. No
c. Not enough information

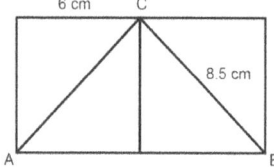

Note: figure not drawn to scale

23. Assuming the 2 quadrangles in the figure above are identical rectangles, what is the perimeter of △ABC in the above shape?

a. 25.5 cm
b. 27 cm
c. 30 cm
d. 29 cm

24. If angle α is equal to the expression 3π/2 - π/6 - π - π/3, find sinα.

a. 0
b. 1/2
c. 1
d. 3/2

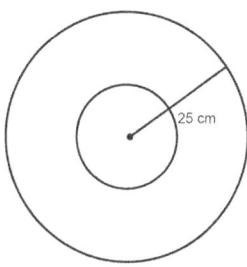

Note: figure not drawn to scale

25. What is the distance travelled by the wheel above, when it makes 175 revolutions?

    a. 87.5 π m
    b. 875 π m
    c. 8.75 π m
    d. 8750 π m

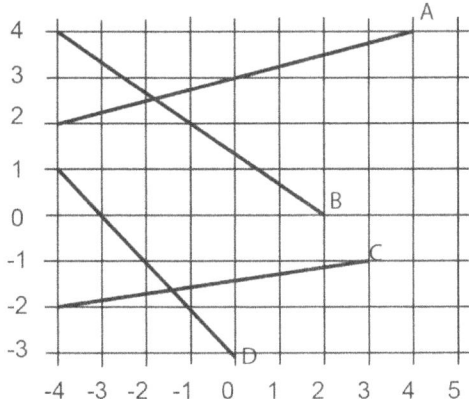

26. Which of the lines above represents the equation 2y − x = 4?

    a. A
    b. B
    c. C
    d. D

27. Find the sides of a right triangle whose sides are consecutive numbers.

    a. 1, 2, 3
    b. 2, 3, 4
    c. 3, 4, 5
    d. 4, 5, 6

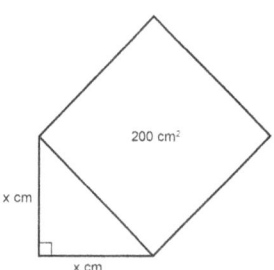

Note: figure not drawn to scale

28. Assuming the quadrangle in the figure above is a square, what is the length of the sides in the triangle above?

    a. 10
    b. 20
    c. 100
    d. 40

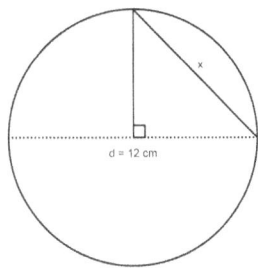

Note: figure not drawn to scale

29. Calculate the length of side x.

    a. 6.46
    b. 8.46
    c. 3.6
    d. 6.4

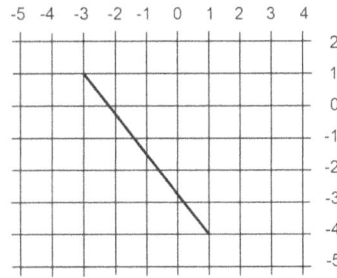

30. What is the slope of the line shown above?

    a. 5/4
    b. -4/5
    c. -5/4
    d. -4/5

WRITING

Directions: For questions 1 - 3, read the short passage answer the question.

Alvin Lee began playing guitar at an early age, and was influenced by his parents' passion for music and inspired by the likes of Chuck Berry and Scotty Moore. [1] Lee started his career as the lead vocalist and guitarist in a band named the Jaybirds at the famous Marquee Club in London in 1962. [2] A few years later the band changed its name to Ten Years After, and released its debut album under the new name. [3] Lee's lightning fast guitar playing at the Woodstock Festival gained him instant stardom and Lee was asked to tour the US. [4]

1. Which sentence in the second paragraph is the least relevant to the main idea of the second paragraph?

    a. 1
    b. 2
    c. 3
    d. 4

Curiosity was launched in late November 2011 from Cape Canaveral Air Force Station in Florida. [1] It successfully landed on Mars on August 6, 2012 searching for evidence of life. [2] The car sized robot, weighing about a ton, is equipped with all the technical capacities to carry out its mission to explore our neighbor for biological, geological and geochemical traces of life. [3] It will also test the Martian soil and surface to collect data about its planetary evolution and surface radiation. [4]

Practice Test Questions 1   45

2. Which sentence is the least relevant to the main idea of the third paragraph?

    a. 1

    b. 2

    c. 3

    d. 4

With an estimated 100,000 species, trees represent 25 percent of all living plant species. Most tree species grow in tropical regions of the world and many of these areas have not been surveyed by botanists, making species diversity poorly understood. The earliest trees were tree ferns and horsetails, which grew in forests in the Carboniferous period. Tree ferns still survive, but the only surviving horsetails are no longer in tree form. Later, in the Triassic period, conifers and ginkgos, appeared, followed by flowering plants after that in the Cretaceous period. [5]

3. Choose the correct list below, ranked from oldest to youngest trees.

    a. Flowering plants, conifers and ginkgos, tree ferns and horsetails

    b. Tree ferns and horsetails, conifers and ginkgos, flowering plants

    c. Tree ferns and horsetails, flowering plants, conifers and ginkgos

    d. Conifers and ginkgos, tree ferns and horsetails, flowering plants

Directions: Choose the word or phrase that best completes the sentence.

4. The Ford Motor Company was named for Henry Ford, _____ had founded the company.

   a. which
   b. who
   c. whose
   d. None of the options are correct.

5. Thomas Edison _____ as the greatest inventor since he invented the light bulb, television, motion pictures, and phonograph.

   a. has always been known
   b. was always been known
   c. must have had been always known
   d. None of the options are correct.

6. The weatherman on Channel 6 said that this has been the _____ summer on record.

   a. most hottest
   b. hottest
   c. hotter
   d. None of the options are correct.

7. Although Joe is tall for his age, his brother Elliot is _____ of the two.

   a. tallest
   b. tall of the two.
   c. the taller
   d. None of the options are correct.

8. When KISS came to town, all the tickets _____ sold out before I could buy one.

   a. will be

   b. had been

   c. were being

   d. None of the options are correct.

9. The rules of most sports _____ more complicated than we often realize.

   a. are

   b. is

   c. was

   d. None of the options are correct.

10. Neither of the Wright Brothers _____ any doubts that they would be successful with their flying machine.

   a. have

   b. has

   c. had

   d. None of the options are correct.

11. The Titanic _____ mere days into its maiden voyage.

   a. will already sunk

   b. sank

   c. had sank

   d. None of the choices are correct.

12. When he's _____ friends, Robert seems confident.

    a. None of the choices are correct.
    b. between
    c. among

13. His home was _____ than we expected.

    a. The sentence is correct.
    b. farther
    c. None of the choices are correct.

14. The tables were _____ by the students.

    a. laid
    b. lay
    c. lie
    d. None of the choices are correct.

15. Each boy and girl _____ given a toy.

    a. were
    b. was
    c. Either A or B can be used.
    d. None of the choices are correct.

16. His measles _____ getting better.

    a. is
    b. are
    c. Either A or B can be used.
    d. None of the choices are correct.

17. Despite the bad weather yesterday, he ___ still attend the party.

    a. The sentence is correct.
    b. could
    c. may
    d. None of the choices are correct.

18. Choose the sentence with the correct punctuation.

    a. To make chicken soup you must first buy a chicken.
    b. To make chicken soup you must first, buy a chicken.
    c. To make chicken soup, you must first buy a chicken.
    d. None of the choices are correct.

19. Choose the sentence with the correct punctuation.

    a. To travel around the globe, you have to drive 25000 miles.
    b. To travel around the globe, you have to drive, 25000 miles.
    c. None of the choices are correct.
    d. To travel around the globe, you have to drive 25,000 miles.

20. Choose the sentence with the correct punctuation.

    a. The dog loved chasing bones, but never ate them; it was running that he enjoyed.
    b. The dog loved chasing bones; but never ate them, it was running that he enjoyed.
    c. The dog loved chasing bones, but never ate them, it was running that he enjoyed.
    d. None of the choices are correct.

21. Choose the sentence with the correct punctuation.

a. However, I believe that he didn't really try that hard.
b. However I believe that he didn't really try that hard.
c. None of the choices are correct.
d. However: I believe that he didn't really try that hard.

22. Choose the sentence that is written correctly.

a. Any girl that fails the test loses their admission.
b. Any girl that fails the test loses our admission.
c. Any girl that fails the test loses <u>her</u> admission.
d. None of the choices are correct.

23. Choose the sentence that is written correctly.

a. He ought to be back by now.
b. He ought be back by now.
c. He ought come back by now.
d. None of the choices are correct.

24. Choose the sentence that is written correctly.

a. The man as well as his son has arrived
b. The man as well as his son have arrived.
c. None of the choices are correct.

25. Choose the sentence that is written correctly.

a. Mark and Peter have talked to each other.
b. Mark and Peter have talked to one another.
c. None of the choices are correct.

26. Choose the sentence that is written correctly.

a. Christians believe that their lord have raised.
b. Christians believe that their lord has risen.
c. Christians believe that their lord have raise.
d. None of the choices are correct.

27. Choose the sentence that is written correctly.

a. Here are the names of people whom you should contact.
b. Here are the names of people who you should contact
c. None of the choices are correct.

28. Choose the sentence that is written correctly.

a. The World Health Organization (WHO) are meeting by January.
b. The World Health Organization (WHO) is meeting by January.
c. None of the choices are correct.

29. Choose the sentence that is written correctly.

a. They will have to retire when they reach 60 years of age.
b. They shall have to retire when they reach 60 years of age.
c. None of the choices are correct.

Directions: Choose the sentence that best support the topic sentence below.

30. Volcanoes occur because the planet's crust is broken into 17 major tectonic plates that float on a hotter, softer layer in the Earth's mantle.

    a. Therefore, volcanoes are generally found where tectonic plates are diverging or converging.

    b. Volcanoes generally cause extensive damage to property.

    c. Volcanoes do not often erupt, but can be spectacular when they do.

    c. Most volcanoes are far from major urban centers.

Answer Key

Section 1 – Reading

1. B
The correct answer because that fact is stated directly in the passage. The passage explains that Anne taught Helen to hear by allowing her to feel the vibrations in her throat.

2. A
We can infer that Anne is a patient teacher because she did not leave or lose her temper when Helen bit or hit her; she just kept trying to teach Helen. Choice B is incorrect because Anne taught Helen to read and talk. Choice C is incorrect because Anne could hear. She was partially blind, not deaf. Choice D is incorrect because it does not have to do with patience.

3. B
The passage states that it was hard for anyone but Anne to understand Helen when she spoke. Choice A is incorrect because the passage does not mention Helen spoke a foreign language. Choice C is incorrect because there is no mention of how quiet or loud Helen's voice was. Choice D is incorrect because we know from reading the passage that Helen did learn to speak.

4. D
This question tests the reader's summarization skills. The other choices A, B, and C focus on portions of the second paragraph that are too narrow and do not relate to the specific portion of text in question. The complexity of the sentence may mislead students into selecting one of these answers, but rearranging or restating the sentence will lead the reader to the correct answer. In addition, choice A makes an assumption that may or may not be true about the intentions of the company, choice B focuses on one product rather than the idea of the products, and choice C makes an assumption about women that may or may not be true and is not supported by the text.

5. D
This question tests the reader's summarization skills. The question is asking very generally about the message of the passage, and the title, "Ways Characters Communicate in Theater," is one indication of that. The other choices A, B, and C are all directly from the text, and therefore readers may be inclined to select one of them, but are too specific to encapsulate the entirety of the passage and its message.

6. B
The paragraph on soliloquies mentions "To be or not to be," and it is from the context of that paragraph that readers may understand that because "To be or not to be" is a soliloquy, Hamlet will be introspective, or thoughtful, while delivering it. It is true that actors deliver soliloquies alone, and may be "solitary" (choice A), but "thoughtful" (choice B) is more true to the overall idea of the paragraph. Readers may choose C because drama and theater can be used interchangeably and the passage mentions that soliloquies are unique to theater (and therefore drama), but this answer is not specific enough to the paragraph in question. Readers may pick up on the theme of life and death and Hamlet's true intentions and select that he is "hopeless" (choice D), but those themes are not discussed either by this paragraph or passage, as a close textual reading and analysis confirms.

7. C
This question tests the reader's grammatical skills. Choice B seems logical, but parenthesis are actually considered to be a stronger break in a sentence than commas are, and along this line of thinking, actually disrupt the sentence more.

Choices A and D make comparisons between theater and film that are simply not made in the passage, and may or may not be true. This detail does clarify the statement that asides are most unique to theater by adding that it is not completely unique to theater, which may have been why the author didn't chose not to delete it and instead used parentheses to designate the detail's importance (choice C).

8. A
Low blood sugar occurs both in diabetics and healthy adults.

9. B
None of the statements are the author's opinion.

10. A
The author's purpose is the inform.

11. A
The only statement that is not a detail is, "A doctor can diagnosis this medical condition by asking the patient questions and testing."

12. A
This sentence is a recommendation.

13. C
Tips for a good night's sleep is the best alternative title for this article.

14. B
Mental activity is helpful for a good night's sleep is cannot be inferred from this article.

15. A
From the passage, one disadvantage of taking naps is they may keep you awake at night.

16. A
Based on the partial table of contents, this book is most likely about how to answer multiple choice.

17. C
To be infamous means to be remembered for an evil or terrible action. Therefore, the word infamy means to remember a bad or terrible thing. Choice A is incorrect because being famous is not the same as being infamous. Choice B is incorrect because the attack on Pearl Harbor was not good. Choice D is incorrect because Pearl Harbor was not forgotten.

18. C
Each answer choice except choice C contains the name of at least one country that was not part of the AXIS powers.

19. D

It is stated in the passage. Choice A is not correct because there was no indication that Japan would attack San Diego. Choice B is incorrect because the attack on Pearl Harbor was a surprise. Choice C is incorrect because Roosevelt was not planning to attack Japan.

20. C

The passage clearly states that Japan planned a surprise attack. They chose that early time to catch the U.S. military off guard. Choice A is incorrect because the military does not sleep late. Choice B is incorrect because there is no law against bombing countries. Choice D is incorrect because it makes no sense.

21. C

This question tests the reader's vocabulary skills. The uses of the negatives "but" and "less," especially right next to each other, may confuse readers into answering with choices A or D, which list words that are antonyms to "militant." Readers may also be confused by the comparison of healthy people with what is being described as an overly healthy person--both people are good, but the reader may look for which one is "worse" in the comparison, and therefore stray toward the antonym words. One key to understanding the meaning of "militant" if the reader is unfamiliar with it is to look at the root of the word; readers can then easily associate it with "military" and gain a sense of what the word signifies: defense (especially considered that the immune system defends the body). Choice C is correct over choice B because "militant" is an adjective, just as the words in choice C are, whereas the words in choice B are nouns.

22. C

This question tests the reader's understanding of function within writing. The other choices are details included surrounding the quoted text, and may therefore confuse the reader. A somewhat contradicts what is said earlier in the paragraph, which is that tests and treatments are improving, and probably doctors are along with them, but the paragraph doesn't actually mention doctors, and the subject of the question is the medicine. Choice B may seem correct to readers who aren't careful to understand that, while the author does mention the large number of people affected, the author is touching on the realities of living with allergies rather about the likelihood of curing all allergies. Similarly, while the author does mention the "balance" of the body, which is easily associated with "wholesome," the author is not really making an argument and especially is not making an extreme statement that allergy medicines should be outlawed. Again, because the article's tone is on living with allergies, choice C is an appropriate choice that fits with the title and content of the text.

23. B
This question tests the reader's inference skills. The text does not state who is doing the recommending, but the use of the "patients," as well as the general context of the passage, lends itself to the logical partner, "doctors," choice B. The author does mention the recommendation but doesn't present it as her own (i.e. "I recommend that"), so choice A may be eliminated. It may seem plausible that people with allergies (choice D) may recommend medicines or products to other people with allergies, but the text does not necessarily support this interaction taking place. Choice C may be selected because the EpiPen is specifically mentioned, but the use of the phrase "such as" when it is introduced is not limiting enough to assume the recommendation is coming from its creators.

24. D
This question tests the reader's global understanding of the text. Choice D includes the main topics of the three body paragraphs, and isn't too focused on a specific aspect or quote from the text, as the other questions are, giving a skewed summary of what the author intended. The reader may be drawn to choice B because of the title of the passage and the use of words like "better," but the message of the passage is larger and more general than this.

25. B
Reading the document posted to the Human Resources website is optional.

26. B
The document is recommended changes and have not be implemented yet.

27. C
This question tests the reader's summarization skills. The use of the word "actually" in describing what kind of people poets are, as well as other moments like this, may lead readers to selecting choices B or D, but the author is more informational than trying to persuade readers. The author gives no indication that she loves poetry (choice B) or that people, students specifically (D), should write poems. Choice A is incorrect because the style and content of this paragraph do not match those of a foreword; forewords usually focus on the history or ideas of a specific poem to introduce it more fully and help it stand out against other poems. The author here focuses on several poems and gives broad statements. Instead, she tells a kind of story about poems, giving three very broad time periods in which to discuss them, thereby giving a brief history of poetry, as choice C states.

28. A
This question tests the reader's summarization skills. Key words in the topic sentences of each of the paragraphs ("oldest," "Renaissance," "modern") should give the reader an idea that the author is moving chronologically. The opening and closing sentence-paragraphs are broad and talk generally. B seems reasonable, but epic poems are mentioned in two paragraphs, eliminating the idea that only new types of poems are used in each paragraph. Choice C is also easily eliminated because the author clearly mentions several different poets, groups of people, and poems. Choice D also seems reasonable, considering that the author does move from older forms of poetry to newer forms, but use of "so (that)" makes this statement false, for the author gives no indication that she is rushing (the paragraphs are about the same size) or that she prefers modern poetry.

29. D
This question tests the reader's attention to detail. The key word is "invented"--it ties together the Mesopotamians, who invented the written word, and the fact that they, as the inventors, also invented and used poetry. The other selections focus on other details mentioned in the passage, such as that the Renaissance's admiration of the Greeks (choice C) and that Beowulf is in Old English (choice A). Choice B may seem like an attractive answer because it is unlike the oth-

ers and because the idea of heroes seems rooted in ancient and early civilizations.

30. B
This question tests the reader's vocabulary and contextualization skills. "Telling" is not an unusual word, but it may be used here in a way that is not familiar to readers, as an adjective rather than a verb in gerund form. A may seem like the obvious answer to a reader looking for a verb to match the use they are familiar with. If the reader understands that the word is being used as an adjective and that choice A is a ploy, they may opt to select choice D, "wordy," but it does not make sense in context. Choice C can be easily eliminated, and doesn't have any connection to the paragraph or passage. "Significant" (choice B) makes sense contextually, especially relative to the phrase "give insight" used later in the sentence.

MATHEMATICS

1. C
243/3 x 3 x 3 = 243/27 = 9

2. B
4y + 24 = 3y + 30, = 4y − 3y + 24 = 30, = y + 24 = 30, = y = 30 − 24, = y = 6

3. B
$(x^2 - y^2) / (x - y) = x + y$

$\dfrac{-(x^2 - xy)}{xy - y^2}$

$\dfrac{-(xy - y^2)}{0}$

4. A
10 x 10 x 100 x 100 = 1000^x, =100 x 10,000 = 1000^x, = 1,000,000 = 1000^x = x = 2

5. C

We are asked to find A + B - C. By paying attention to the sign distribution; we write the polynomials and operate:

A + B - C = $(-2x^4 + x^2 - 3x) + (x^4 - x^3 + 5) - (x^4 + 2x^3 + 4x + 5)$

= $-2x^4 + x^2 - 3x + x^4 - x^3 + 5 - x^4 - 2x^3 - 4x - 5$

= $-2x^4 + x^4 - x^4 - x^3 - 2x^3 + x^2 - 3x - 4x + 5 - 5$ ... similar terms written together to ease summing/substituting.

= $-2x^4 - 3x^3 + x^2 - 7x$

6. C

To find the solution for the inequality, we need to simplify it first:

$(x - 6)^2 \geq x^2 + 12$ ... we can write the open form of the left side:

$x^2 - 12x + 36 \geq x^2 + 12$ ... x^2 terms on both sides cancel each other:

$-12x + 36 \geq 12$ ... Now, we aim to have x alone on one side. So, we subtract 36 from both sides:

$-12x + 36 - 36 \geq 12 - 36$

$-12x \geq -24$ ... We divide both sides by -12. This means that the inequality will change its direction:

$x \leq 2$ ... x can be 2 or a smaller value.

This result is shown by $(-\infty, 2]$.

7. B

(7 x 7 x 7 x 7 x 7) - (3 x 3 x 3 x 3 x 3) = 16,807 – 243 = 16,564.

8. C

$(x^3 - 3x^2 + 3x - 1) / (x - 1) = x^2 - 2x + 1$
<u>-($x^3 - x^2$)</u>
    $-2x^2 + 3x - 1$
    <u>-(-2x^2 + 2x)</u>
            x - 1

<u>-(x - 1)</u>
0

9. C
Exponential form is 9^3 and standard from is 729

10. B
$x^2 - 5x - 6 = 0$

We try to separate the middle term -5x to find common factors with x^2 and -6 separately:

$x^2 - 6x + x - 6 = 0$ ... Here, we see that x is a common factor for x^2 and -6x:

$x(x - 6) + x - 6 = 0$ ... Here, we have x times x - 6 and 1 time x - 6 summed up. This means that we have x + 1 times x - 6:

$(x + 1)(x - 6) = 0$ ... This is true when either or both of the expressions in the parenthesis are equal to zero:

$x + 1 = 0$ ... $x = -1$

$x - 6 = 0$ ... $x = 6$

-1 and 6 are the solutions for this quadratic equation.

11. B
$0.524/ (10 * 10 * 10) = 0.524/1000$ ... This means that we need to carry the decimal point 3 decimals left from the point it is now:

= 0.0.0.0.524 = 0.000524

12. A
We need to find the greatest common divisor of the two terms in order to factor the expression. We should remember that if the bases of exponent numbers are the same, the multiplication of two terms is found by summing the powers and writing on the same base. Similarly; when dividing, the power of the divisor is subtracted from the power of the divided.
Both x^3y^3 and x^2y^8 contain x^2 and y^3. So;

$x^3y^3 - x^2y^8 = x * x^2y^3 - y^5 * x^2y^3$ ... We can carry x^2y^3 out as the factor:

$= x^2y^3(x - y^5$

13. D
Our aim is to collect the knowns on one side, and the unknowns (x terms) on the other side:

$5x/2 = (3x + 24)/6$ ... First, we can simplify the denominators of both sides by 2:

$5x = (3x + 24)/3$ ... Now, we can do cross multiplication:

$15x = 3x + 24$

$15x - 3x = 24$

$12x = 24$

$x = 24/12 = 2$

14. D
When multiplying exponents with the same base, add the exponents. $3^2 \times 3^5 = 3^{2+5} = 3^7$

15. C
Solving the system means finding x and y. Since we also have a in the system, we will find x and y depending on a.

We can obtain y by using the equation $ax + y = 1$:

$y = 1 - ax$ ... Then, we can insert this value into the second equation:

$x + a(1 - ax) = 1$

$x + a - a^2x = 1$

$x - a^2x = 1 - a$

$x(1 - a^2) = 1 - a$ ... We need to obtain x alone:

$x = (1 - a)/(1 - a^2)$ ... Here, $1 - a^2 = (1 - a)(1 + a)$ is used:

$x = (1 - a)/((1 - a)(1 + a))$ ... Simplifying by $(1 - a)$:

$x = 1/(a + 1)$ ... Now we know the value of x. By using either of the equations, we can find the value of y. Let us use $y = 1 - ax$:

$y = 1 - a * 1/(a + 1)$

y = 1 - a/(a + 1) ... By writing on the same denominator:

y = ((a + 1) - a)/(a + 1)

y = (a + 1 - a)/(a + 1) ... a and -a cancel each other:

y = 1/(a + 1) ... x and y are found to be equal.

The solution of the system is (1/(a + 1), 1/(a + 1))

16. A
To divide exponents with the same base, subtract the exponents. $3^{8-5} = 3^3$

17. C
To solve the linear equation, we operate the knowns and unknowns within each other and try to obtain x term (which is the unknown) alone on one side of the equation:

3(x + 2) - 2(1 - x) = 4x + 5 ... We remove the parenthesis by distributing the factors:

3x + 6 - 2 + 2x = 4x + 5

5x + 4 = 4x + 5

5x - 4x = 5 - 4

x = 1

18. C
$3x^a + 6a^x - x^a + (-5a^x) - 2x^a = 3x^a + 6a^x - x^a - 5a^x - 2x^a = a^x$

19. B
By paying attention to the sign distribution; we write the polynomials and operate:
$(-3x^2 + 2x + 6) + (-x^2 - x - 1)$

$= -3x^2 + 2x + 6 - x^2 - x - 1$

$= -3x^2 - x^2 + 2x - x + 6 - 1$ ... similar terms written together to ease summing/substituting.

$= -4x^2 + x + 5$

20. A
10^4 is not equal to 100,000
$10^4 = 10 \times 10 \times 10 \times 10 = 10^2 \times 10^2 = 10,000$

21. D
Comparing angles on similar triangles, a, b and c will be 70°, 35°, 35°

22. A
Yes the triangles are congruent.

23. D
Perimeter of triangle ABC is asked.
Perimeter of a triangle = sum of all three sides.

Here, Perimeter of $\triangle ABC$ = |AC| + |CB| + |AB|.

Since the triangle is located in the middle of two adjacent and identical rectangles, we find the side lengths using these rectangles:

|AB| = 6 + 6 = 12 cm

|CB| = 8.5 cm

|AC| = |CB| = 8.5 cm

Perimeter = |AC| + |CB| + |AB| = 8.5 + 8.5 + 12 = 29 cm

24. A
First, we need to simplify the value of angle α:

α = 3π/2 - π/6 - π - π/3 ... by equating the denominators at 6:

α = 9π/6 - π/6 - 6π/6 - 2π/6

α = (9 - 1 - 6 - 2)π/6

α = 0 * π /6

α = 0

sinα = sin0° = 0

25. A
The wheel travels 2πr distance when it makes one revolution. Here, r stands for the radius. The radius is given as 25 cm in the figure. So,
2πr = 2π * 25 = 50π cm is the distance travelled in one revolution.

In 175 revolutions: 175 * 50π = 8750π cm is travelled.

We are asked to find the distance in meter.

1 m = 100 cm So;

8750π cm = 8750π / 100 = 87.5π m

26. A
If a line represents an equation, all points on that line should satisfy the equation. Meaning that all (x, y) pairs present on the line should be able to verify that 2y - x is equal to 4. We can find out the correct line by trying a (x, y) point existing on each line. It is easier to choose points on the intersection of the gridlines:
Let us try the point (4, 4) on line A:

2 * 4 - 4 = 4

8 - 4 = 4

4 = 4 ... this is a correct result, so the equation for line A is 2y - x = 4.

Let us try other points to check the other lines:

Point (-1, 2) on line B:

2 * 2 - (-1) = 4

4 + 1 = 4

5 = 4 ... this is a wrong result, so the equation for line B is not 2y - x = 4.

Point (3, -1) on line C:

2 * (-1) - 3 = 4

-2 - 3 = 4

-5 = 4 ... this is a wrong result, so the equation for line C is not 2y - x = 4.

Point (-2, -1) on line D:

2 * (-1) - (-2) = 4

-2 + 2 = 4

0 = 4 ... this is a wrong result, so the equation for line D is not 2y - x = 4.

27. C
In a right angle, Pythagorean Theorem is applicable:
$a^2 + b^2 = c^2$ ... Here, a and b represent the adjacent and opposite sides, c represents the hypotenuse. Hypotenuse is larger than the other two sides.

In this question, we need to try each answer choice by applying $a^2 + b^2 = c^2$ to see if it is satisfied; by inserting the largest number into c:

a. 1, 2, 3:

$1^2 + 2^2 = 3^2$

1 + 4 = 9

5 = 9 ... This is not correct, so answer choice does not represent a right angle whose sides are consecutive numbers.

b. 2, 3, 4:

$2^2 + 3^2 = 4^2$

4 + 9 = 16

13 = 16 ... This is not correct, so this answer choice does not represent a right angle whose sides are consecutive numbers.

c. 3, 4, 5:

$3^2 + 4^2 = 5^2$

$9 + 16 = 25$

$25 = 25$ ... This is correct, 3, 4, 5 are also consecutive numbers; so this answer choice represents a right angle whose sides are consecutive numbers.

d. 4, 5, 6:

$4^2 + 5^2 = 6^2$

$16 + 25 = 36$

$41 = 36$ ... This is not correct, so this answer choice does not represent a right angle whose sides are consecutive numbers.

28. A
If we call one side of the square "a," the area of the square will be a^2.

We know that $a^2 = 200$ cm².

On the other hand; there is an isosceles right triangle.

Pythagorean Theorem:
(Hypotenuse)² = (Perpendicular)² + (Base)²
$h^2 = a^2 + b^2$

Given: $h^2 = 200$, $a = b = x$
Then, $x^2 + x^2 = 200$, $2x^2 = 200$, $x^2 = 100$
$x = 10$

29. B
In the question, we have a right triangle formed inside the circle. We are asked to find the length of the hypotenuse of this triangle. We can find the other two sides of the triangle by using circle properties:

The diameter of the circle is equal to 12 cm. The legs of the right triangle are the radii of the circle; so they are 6 cm long.

Pythagorean Theorem:
(Hypotenuse)² = (Perpendicular)² + (Base)²
$h^2 = a^2 + b^2$

Given: d (diameter)= 12 & r (radius) = a = b = 6
$h^2 = a^2 + b^2$
$h^2 = 6^2 + 6^2$, $h^2 = 36 + 36$
$h^2 = 72$
h = 8.46

30. C
Slope (m) = change in y / change in x

(x_1, y_1)=(-3,1) & (x_2, y_2)= (1,-4)
Slope = [-4 - 1]/[1-(-3)]= -5/4

WRITING

1. A
Sentence 1 is least relevant, "Alvin Lee began playing guitar at an early age, and was influenced by his parents' passion for music and inspired by the likes of Chuck Berry and Scotty Moore."
This sentence talks about Lee's motivation rather than his achievements, which is the main topic of the paragraph. Other sentences are related to a significant extent, but this sentence deviates from the main idea the most.

2. A
Sentence 1 is the least relevant. "Curiosity was launched in late November 2011 from Cape Canaveral Air Force Station in Florida."

This paragraph talks about the objectives of the rover. All sentences other than sentence 2 mention the objectives. This sentence, however, informs us when the spacecraft was launched.

3. B
Here is the passage with the oldest to youngest trees

The earliest trees were [1] tree ferns and horsetails, which grew in forests in the Carboniferous period. Tree ferns still survive, but the only surviving horsetails are no longer in tree form. Later, in the Triassic period, [2] conifers and ginkgos, appeared, [3] followed by flowering plants after that in the Cretaceous period

4. B
The sentence refers to a person, so "who" is the only correct choice.

5. A
The sentence requires the past perfect "has always been known." The clue to this tense is the use of "since."

6. B
The superlative, "hottest," is used when expressing a temperature greater than that of anything to which it is being compared.

7. C
When comparing two items, use "the taller." When comparing more than two items, use "the tallest."

8. B
The past perfect form is used to describe an event that occurred in the past and before another event.

9. A
The subject is "rules" so the present tense plural form, "are," is used to agree with "realize."

10. C
The simple past tense, "had," is correct because it refers to completed action in the past.

11. B
The simple past tense, "sank," is correct because it refers to completed action in the past.

12. C
Among vs. Between. 'Among' is for more than 2 items, and 'between' is only for 2 items.

When he's among friends (many or more than 2), Robert seems confident, but, between you and me (two), he is very shy.

13. B
Further vs. Farther. 'Farther' is used for physical distance, and 'further' is used for figurative distance.

14. A
The verb "lay" should always take an object. Here the subject is the table. The three forms of the verb lay are: lay, laid and laid. The sentence above is in past tense.

15. B
Use the singular verb form when nouns are qualified with "every" or "each," even if they are joined by 'and. '

16. B
Use a plural verb for nouns like measles, tongs, trousers, riches, scissors etc.

17. B
Use "could," the past tense of "can" to express ability or capacity.

18. C
Comma separate phrases.

19. D
The comma separates clauses and numbers are separated with a comma. The correct sentence is,
'To travel around the globe, you have to drive 25,000 miles.'

20. A
The dog loved chasing bones, but never ate them; it was running that he enjoyed.

21. A
When using 'however,' place a comma before and after, except when however begins the sentence.

22. C
Words such as neither, each, many, either, every, everyone,

everybody and any should take a singular pronoun.

23. A
The verb "ought" can be used to express desirability, duty and probability. The verb is usually followed by "to."

24. A
When two subjects are linked with "with" or "as well," use the verb form that matches the first subject.

25. A
When you use 'each other' it should be used for two things or people. When you use 'one another' it should be used for things and people above two

26. B
The verb rise ('to go up', 'to ascend.') can appear in three forms, rise, rose, and risen. The verb should not take an object.

27. A
The sentence is correct. Use "whom" in the objective case, and use "who" a subjective case.

28. B
Use a singular verb with a proper noun in plural form that refers to a single entity. Here, the The World Health Organization is a single entity, although it is made up on many members.

29. A
Will is used in the second or third person (they, he, she and you), while shall is used in the first person (I and we). Both verbs are used to express futurity.

30. A
Sentence A continues directly the discussion about tectonic plates. The other choices diverge from this central idea.

PRACTICE TEST QUESTIONS SET 2

The questions below are not the same as you will find on the PERT - that would be too easy! And nobody knows what the questions will be and they change all the time. Below are general questions that cover the same subject areas as the PERT. So, while the format and exact wording of the questions may differ slightly, and change from year to year, if you can answer the questions below, you will have no problem with the PERT.

For the best results, take these practice test questions as if it were the real exam. Set aside time when you will not be disturbed, and a location that is quiet and free of distractions. Read the instructions carefully, read each question carefully, and answer to the best of your ability.
Use the bubble answer sheets provided. When you have completed the Practice Questions, check your answer against the Answer Key and read the explanation provided.

Do not attempt more than one set of practice test questions in one day. After completing the first practice test, wait two or three days before attempting the second set of questions.

Reading Answer Sheet

	A	B	C	D	E		A	B	C	D	E
1	○	○	○	○	○	21	○	○	○	○	○
2	○	○	○	○	○	22	○	○	○	○	○
3	○	○	○	○	○	23	○	○	○	○	○
4	○	○	○	○	○	24	○	○	○	○	○
5	○	○	○	○	○	25	○	○	○	○	○
6	○	○	○	○	○	26	○	○	○	○	○
7	○	○	○	○	○	27	○	○	○	○	○
8	○	○	○	○	○	28	○	○	○	○	○
9	○	○	○	○	○	29	○	○	○	○	○
10	○	○	○	○	○	30	○	○	○	○	○
11	○	○	○	○	○						
12	○	○	○	○	○						
13	○	○	○	○	○						
14	○	○	○	○	○						
15	○	○	○	○	○						
16	○	○	○	○	○						
17	○	○	○	○	○						
18	○	○	○	○	○						
19	○	○	○	○	○						
20	○	○	○	○	○						

Mathematics Answer Sheet

	A	B	C	D	E		A	B	C	D	E
1	○	○	○	○	○	21	○	○	○	○	○
2	○	○	○	○	○	22	○	○	○	○	○
3	○	○	○	○	○	23	○	○	○	○	○
4	○	○	○	○	○	24	○	○	○	○	○
5	○	○	○	○	○	25	○	○	○	○	○
6	○	○	○	○	○	26	○	○	○	○	○
7	○	○	○	○	○	27	○	○	○	○	○
8	○	○	○	○	○	28	○	○	○	○	○
9	○	○	○	○	○	29	○	○	○	○	○
10	○	○	○	○	○	30	○	○	○	○	○
11	○	○	○	○	○						
12	○	○	○	○	○						
13	○	○	○	○	○						
14	○	○	○	○	○						
15	○	○	○	○	○						
16	○	○	○	○	○						
17	○	○	○	○	○						
18	○	○	○	○	○						
19	○	○	○	○	○						
20	○	○	○	○	○						

Writing Skills Answer Sheet

	A	B	C	D	E		A	B	C	D	E
1	○	○	○	○	○	21	○	○	○	○	○
2	○	○	○	○	○	22	○	○	○	○	○
3	○	○	○	○	○	23	○	○	○	○	○
4	○	○	○	○	○	24	○	○	○	○	○
5	○	○	○	○	○	25	○	○	○	○	○
6	○	○	○	○	○	26	○	○	○	○	○
7	○	○	○	○	○	27	○	○	○	○	○
8	○	○	○	○	○	28	○	○	○	○	○
9	○	○	○	○	○	29	○	○	○	○	○
10	○	○	○	○	○	30	○	○	○	○	○
11	○	○	○	○	○						
12	○	○	○	○	○						
13	○	○	○	○	○						
14	○	○	○	○	○						
15	○	○	○	○	○						
16	○	○	○	○	○						
17	○	○	○	○	○						
18	○	○	○	○	○						
19	○	○	○	○	○						
20	○	○	○	○	○						

Part 1 – Reading and Language Arts

Questions 1 - 4 refer to the following passage.

Passage 1 - The Crusades

In 1095 Pope Urban II proclaimed the First Crusade with the intent and stated goal to restore Christian access to holy places in and around Jerusalem. Over the next 200 years there were 6 major crusades and numerous minor crusades in the fight for control of the "Holy Land." Historians are divided on the real purpose of the Crusades, some believing that it was part of a purely defensive war against Islamic conquest; some see them as part of a long-running conflict at the frontiers of Europe; and others see them as confident, aggressive, papal-led expansion attempts by Western Christendom. The impact of the crusades was profound, and judgment of the Crusaders ranges from laudatory to highly critical. However, all agree that the Crusades and wars waged during those crusades were brutal and often bloody. Several hundred thousand Roman Catholic Christians joined the Crusades, they were Christians from all over Europe.

Europe at the time was under the Feudal System, so while the Crusaders made vows to the Church they also were beholden to their Feudal Lords. This led to the Crusaders not only fighting the Saracen, the commonly used word for Muslim at the time, but also each other for power and economic gain in the Holy Land. This infighting between the Crusaders is why many historians hold the view that the Crusades were simply a front for Europe to invade the Holy Land for economic gain in the name of the Church. Another factor contributing to this theory is that while the army of crusaders marched towards Jerusalem they pillaged the land as they went. The church and feudal Lords vowing to return the land to its original beauty, and inhabitants, this rarely happened though as the Lords often kept the land for themselves. A full 800 years after the Crusades, Pope John Paul II expressed his sorrow for the massacre of innocent people and the lasting damage the Medieval church caused in that area of the World.

1. What is the tone of this article?

a. Subjective
b. Objective
c. Persuasive
d. None of the Above

2. What can all historians agree on concerning the Crusades?

a. It achieved great things
b. It stabilized the Holy Land
c. It was bloody and brutal
d. It helped defend Europe from the Byzantine Empire

3. What impact did the feudal system have on the Crusades?

a. It unified the Crusaders
b. It helped gather volunteers
c. It had no effect on the Crusades
d. It led to infighting, causing more damage than good

4. What does Saracen mean?

a. Muslim
b. Christian
c. Knight
d. Holy Land

Questions 5 - 8 refer to the following passage.

ABC Electric Warranty

ABC Electric Company warrants that its products are free from defects in material and workmanship. Subject to the conditions and limitations set forth below, ABC Electric will, at its option, either repair or replace any part of its products that prove defective due to improper workmanship or materials.

This limited warranty does not cover any damage to the product from improper installation, accident, abuse, misuse, natural disaster, insufficient or excessive electrical supply, abnormal mechanical or environmental conditions, or any unauthorized disassembly, repair, or modification.

This limited warranty also does not apply to any product on which the original identification information has been altered, or removed, has not been handled or packaged correctly, or has been sold as second-hand.

This limited warranty covers only repair, replacement, refund or credit for defective ABC Electric products, as provided above.

5. I tried to repair my ABC Electric blender, but could not, so can I get it repaired under this warranty?

    a. Yes, the warranty still covers the blender

    b. No, the warranty does not cover the blender

    c. Uncertain. ABC Electric may or may not cover repairs under this warranty

6. My ABC Electric fan is not working. Will ABC Electric provide a new one or repair this one?

    a. ABC Electric will repair my fan

    b. ABC Electric will replace my fan

    c. ABC Electric could either replace or repair my fan can request either a replacement or a repair.

7. My stove was damaged in a flood. Does this warranty cover my stove?

   a. Yes, it is covered.
   b. No, it is not covered.
   c. It may or may not be covered.
   d. ABC Electric will decide if it is covered

8. Which of the following is an example of improper workmanship?

   a. Missing parts
   b. Defective parts
   c. Scratches on the front
   d. None of the above

Questions 9 – 12 refer to the following passage.

Passage 2 - Women and Advertising

Only in the last few generations have media messages been so widespread and so readily seen, heard, and read by so many people. Advertising is an important part of both selling and buying anything from soap to cereal to jeans. For whatever reason, more consumers are women than are men. Media message are subtle but powerful, and more attention has been paid lately to how these message affect women. Of all the products that women buy, makeup, clothes, and other stylistic or cosmetic products are among the most popular. This means that companies focus their advertising on women, promising them that their product will make her feel, look, or smell better than the next company's product will. This competition has resulted in advertising that is more and more ideal and less and less possible for everyday women. However, because women do look to these ideals and the products they represent as how they can potentially become, many women have developed unhealthy attitudes about themselves when they have failed to become those ideals.

In recent years, more companies have tried to change advertisements to be healthier for women. This includes featuring models of more sizes and addressing a huge outcry against unfair tools such as airbrushing and photo editing. There is debate about what the right balance between real and ideal is, because fashion is also considered art and some changes are made to purposefully elevate fashionable products and signify that they are creative, innovative, and the work of individual people. Artists want their freedom protected as much as women do, and advertising agencies are often caught in the middle.

Some claim that the companies who make these changes are not doing enough. Many people worry that there are still not enough models of different sizes and different ethnicities. Some people claim that companies use this healthier type of advertisement not for the good of women, but because they would like to sell products to the women who are looking for these kinds of messages. This is also a hard balance to find: companies do need to make money, and women do need to feel respected.

While the focus of this change has been on women, advertising can also affect men, and this change will hopefully be a lesson on media for all consumers.

9. The second paragraph states that advertising focuses on women

     a. to shape what the ideal should be

     b. because women buy makeup

     c. because women are easily persuaded

     d. because of the types of products that women buy

10. According to the passage, fashion artists and female consumers are at odds because

   a. there is a debate going on and disagreement drives people apart

   b. both of them are trying to protect their freedom to do something

   c. artists want to elevate their products above the reach of women

   d. women are creative, innovative, individual people

11. The author uses the phrase "for whatever reason" in this passage to

   a. keep the focus of the paragraph on media messages and not on the differences between men and women

   b. show that the reason for this is unimportant

   c. argue that it is stupid that more women are consumers than men

   d. show that he or she is tired of talking about why media messages are important

12. This passage suggests that

   a. advertising companies are still working on making their messages better

   b. all advertising companies seek to be more approachable for women

   c. women are only buying from companies that respect them

   d. artists could stop producing fashionable products if they feel bullied

Questions 13 - 16 refer to the following passage.

FDR, the Treaty of Versailles, and the Fourteen Points

At the conclusion of World War I, those who had won the war and those who were forced to admit defeat welcomed the end of the war and expected that a peace treaty would be signed. The American president, Franklin D. Roosevelt, played an important part in proposing what the agreements should be and did so through his Fourteen Points.
World War I had begun in 1914 when an Austrian archduke was assassinated, leading to a domino effect that pulled the world's most powerful countries into war on a large scale. The war catalyzed the creation and use of deadly weapons that had not previously existed, resulting in a great loss of soldiers on both sides of the fighting. More than 9 million soldiers were killed.

The United States agreed to enter the war right before it ended, and many believed that its decision to become finally involved brought on the end of the war. FDR made it very clear that the U.S. was entering the war for moral reasons and had an agenda focused on world peace. The Fourteen Points were individual goals and ideas (focused on peace, free trade, open communication, and self reliance) that FDR wanted the power nations to strive for now that the war had concluded. He was optimistic and had many ideas about what could be accomplished through and during the post-war peace. However, FDR's fourteen points were poorly received when he presented them to the leaders of other world powers, many of whom wanted only to help their own countries and to punish the Germans for fueling the war, and they fell by the wayside. World War II was imminent, for Germany lost everything.

Some historians believe that the other leaders who participated in the Treaty of Versailles weren't receptive to the Fourteen Points because World War I was fought almost entirely on European soil, and the United States lost much less than did the other powers. FDR was in a unique position to determine the fate of the war, but doing it on his own terms did not help accomplish his goals. This is only one historical example of how the United State has tried to use its power as an important country, but found itself limited because of geological or ideological factors.

13. The main idea of this passage is that

    a. World War I was unfair because no fighting took place in America

    b. World War II happened because of the Treaty of Versailles

    c. the power the United States has to help other countries also prevents it from helping other countries

    d. Franklin D. Roosevelt was one of the United States' smartest presidents

14. According to the second paragraph, World War I started because

    a. an archduke was assassinated

    b. weapons that were more deadly had been developed

    c. a domino effect of allies agreeing to help each other

    d. the world's most powerful countries were large

15. The author includes the detail that 9 million soldiers were killed

    a. to demonstrate why European leaders were hesitant to accept peace

    b. to show the reader the dangers of deadly weapons

    c. to make the reader think about which countries lost the most soldiers

    d. to demonstrate why World War II was imminent

16. According to this passage, it can be understood that the word catalyzed means

a. analyzed
b. sped up
c. invented
d. funded

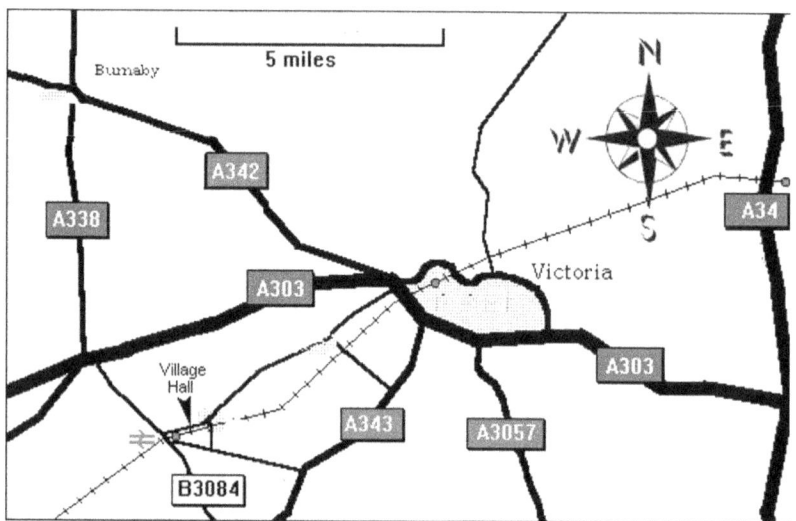

17. Approximately how far is Victoria to Burnaby?

a. About 10 miles
b. About 5 miles
c. About 15 miles
d. About 20 miles

18. How is the Village Hall from Victoria?

a. About 10 miles
b. About 5 miles
c. About 15 miles
d. About 20 miles

Questions 19 - 22 refer to the following passage.

Chocolate Chip Cookies

3/4 cup sugar
3/4 cup packed brown sugar
1 cup butter, softened
2 large eggs, beaten
1 teaspoon vanilla extract
2 1/4 cups all-purpose flour
1 teaspoon baking soda
3/4 teaspoon salt
2 cups semisweet chocolate chips
If desired, 1 cup chopped pecans, or chopped walnuts.
Preheat oven to 375 degrees.

Mix sugar, brown sugar, butter, vanilla and eggs in a large bowl. Stir in flour, baking soda, and salt. The dough will be very stiff.

Stir in chocolate chips by hand with a sturdy wooden spoon. Add the pecans, or other nuts, if desired. Stir until the chocolate chips and nuts are evenly dispersed.

Drop dough by rounded tablespoonfuls 2 inches apart onto a cookie sheet.

Bake 8 to 10 minutes or until light brown. Cookies may look underdone, but they will finish cooking after you take them out of the oven.

19. What is the correct order for adding these ingredients?

    a. Brown sugar, baking soda, chocolate chips
    b. Baking soda, brown sugar, chocolate chips
    c. Chocolate chips, baking soda, brown sugar
    d. Baking soda, chocolate chips, brown sugar

20. What does sturdy mean?

   a. Long

   b. Strong

   c. Short

   d. Wide

21. What does disperse mean?

   a. Scatter

   b. To form a ball

   c. To stir

   d. To beat

22. When can you stop stirring the nuts?

   a. When the cookies are cooked.

   b. When the nuts are evenly distributed.

   c. When the nuts are added.

   d. After the chocolate chips are added.

Questions 23 - 26 refer to the following passage.

Passage 5 - Frankenstein

Great God! What a scene has just taken place! I am yet dizzy with the remembrance of it. I hardly know whether I shall have the power to detail it; yet the tale which I have recorded would be incomplete without this final and wonderful catastrophe. I entered the cabin where lay the remains of my ill-fated and admirable friend. Over him hung a form which I cannot find words to describe—gigantic in stature, yet uncouth and distorted in its proportions. As he hung over the coffin, his face was concealed by long locks of ragged hair; but one vast hand was extended, in color and apparent texture like that of a mummy. When he heard the sound of my approach, he ceased to utter exclamations of grief and horror and sprung towards the window. Never did I behold a vision so horrible as his face, of such loathsome yet appalling hideousness. I shut my eyes involuntarily and endeavored to recollect what were my duties with regard to this destroyer. I called on him to stay.

He paused, looking on me with wonder, and again turning towards the lifeless form of his creator, he seemed to forget my presence, and every feature and gesture seemed instigated by the wildest rage of some uncontrollable passion.

"That is also my victim!" he exclaimed. "In his murder my crimes are consummated; the miserable series of my being is wound to its close! Oh, Frankenstein! Generous and self-devoted being! What does it avail that I now ask thee to pardon me? I, who irretrievably destroyed thee by destroying all thou lovedst. Alas! He is cold, he cannot answer me."

His voice seemed suffocated, and my first impulses, which had suggested to me the duty of obeying the dying request of my friend in destroying his enemy, were now suspended by a mixture of curiosity and compassion. I approached this tremendous being; I dared not again raise my eyes to his face, there was something so scaring and unearthly in his ugliness. I attempted to speak, but the words died away on my lips. The monster continued to utter wild and incoherent self-reproaches. At length I gathered resolution to address him in a pause of the tempest of his passion.

"Your repentance," I said, "is now superfluous. If you had listened to the voice of conscience and heeded the stings of remorse before you had urged your diabolical vengeance to this extremity, Frankenstein would yet have lived." [7]

23. Who is the "ill-fated and admirable friend" who is lying in the coffin?

    a. Frankenstein's monster

    b. Frankenstein

    c. Mary Shelley

    d. Unknown

24. Why is the speaker 'suspended" from following through on his duty to destroy the monster?

a. The way the monster looks

b. The monster's remorse

c. Curiosity and compassion

d. Fear the monster might kill him too

25. How does Frankenstein's monster destroy Frankenstein?

a. By killing Frankenstein

b. By letting himself be the monster everyone sees him as

c. By destroying everything Frankenstein loved

d. All of the above

26. When the Speaker says the monster's repentance is "superfluous, what does he mean?

a. That it is unnecessary and unused because Frankenstein is already dead and cannot hear him

b. That he accepts the repentance on behalf of Frankenstein

c. That the monster does not actually feel remorseful

d. That his repentance is unneeded because he did not do anything wrong

Questions 27 - 30 refer to the following passage.

Lowest Price Guarantee

Get it for less. Guaranteed!

ABC Electric will beat any advertised price by 10% of the difference.

1) If you find a lower advertised price, we will beat it by 10% of the difference.

2) If you find a lower advertised price within 30 days* of your purchase we will beat it by 10% of the difference.

3) If our own price is reduced within 30 days* of your purchase, bring in your receipt and we will refund the difference.

*14 days for computers, monitors, printers, laptops, tablets, cellular & wireless devices, home security products, projectors, camcorders, digital cameras, radar detectors, portable DVD players, DJ and pro-audio equipment, and air conditioners.

27. I bought a radar detector 15 days ago and saw an ad for the same model only cheaper. Can I get 10% of the difference refunded?

    a. Yes. Since it is less than 30 days, you can get 10% of the difference refunded.

    b. No. Since it is more than 14 days, you cannot get 10% of the difference re-funded.

    c. It depends on the cashier.

    d. Yes. You can get the difference refunded.

28. I bought a flat-screen TV for $500 10 days ago and found an advertisement for the same TV, at another store, on sale for $400. How much will ABC refund under this guarantee?

    a. $100
    b. $110
    c. $10
    d. $400

29. What is the purpose of this passage?

    a. To inform
    b. To educate
    c. To persuade
    d. To entertain

Questions 30 refers to the following passage.

Passage 6 - What Is Mardi Gras?

Mardi Gras is fast becoming one of the South's most famous and most celebrated holidays. The word Mardi Gras comes from the French and the literal translation is "Fat Tuesday." The holiday has also been called Shrove Tuesday, due to its associations with Lent. The purpose of Mardi Gras is to celebrate and enjoy before the Lenten season of fasting and repentance begins.

What originated by the French Explorers in New Orleans, Louisiana in the 17th century is now celebrated all over the world. Panama, Italy, Belgium and Brazil all host large scale Mardi Gras celebrations, and many smaller cities and towns celebrate this fun loving Tuesday as well. Usually held in February or early March, Mardi Gras is a day of extravagance, a day for people to eat, drink and be merry, to wear costumes, masks and to dance to jazz music.
The French explorers on the Mississippi River would be in shock today if they saw the opulence of the parades and floats that grace the New Orleans streets during Mardi Gras these days. Parades in New Orleans are divided by organizations. These are more commonly known as Krewes.

Being a member of a Krewe is quite a task because Krewes are responsible for overseeing the parades. Each Krewe's parade is ruled by a Mardi Gras "King and Queen." The role of the King and Queen is to "bestow" gifts on their adoring fans as the floats ride along the street. They throw doubloons, which is fake money and usually colored green, purple and gold, which are the colors of Mardi Gras. Beads in those color shades are also thrown and cups are thrown as well. Beads are by far the most popular souvenir of any Mardi Gras parade, with each spectator attempting to gather as many as possible.

30. The purpose of Mardi Gras is to

    a. Repent for a month.

    b. Celebrate in extravagant ways.

    c. Be a member of a Krewe.

    d. Explore the Mississippi.

MATHEMATICS

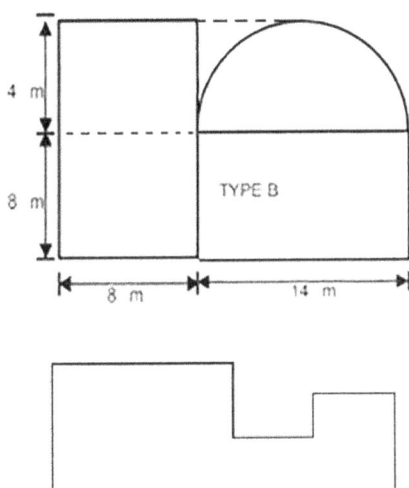

Type A: 1300 ft²

1. The price of houses in a certain subdivision is based on the total area. Susan is watching her budget and wants to choose the house with the lowest area. Which house type, A (1300 ft2) or B, should she choose if she would like the house with the lowest price? (1cm² = 4.0ft² & π = 22/7)

    a. Type B is smaller 140 ft²

    b. Type A is smaller

    c. Type B is smaller at 855 ft²

    d. Type B is larger

2. Using the quadratic formula, solve the quadratic equation: $0.9x^2 + 1.8x - 2.7 = 0$

    a. 1 and 3

    b. -3 and 1

    c. -3 and -1

    d. -1 and 3

3. Subtract polynomials $4x^3 - 2x^2 - 10$ and $5x^3 + x^2 + x + 5$.

    a. $-x^3 - 3x^2 - x - 15$

    b. $9x^3 - 3x^2 - x - 15$

    c. $-x^3 - x^2 + x - 5$

    d. $9x^3 - x^2 + x + 5$

4. Find x and y from the following system of equations:

$(4x + 5y)/3 = ((x - 3y)/2) + 4$
$(3x + y)/2 = ((2x + 7y)/3) - 1$

    a. (1, 3)

    b. (2, 1)

    c. (1, 1)

    d. (0, 1)

Practice Test Questions 2

5. Using the factoring method, solve the quadratic equation: $x^2 + 12x - 13 = 0$

    a. -13 and 1
    b. -13 and -1
    c. 1 and 13
    d. -1 and 13

6. Using the quadratic formula, solve the quadratic equation:

$$\frac{x+2}{x-2} + \frac{x-2}{x+2} = 0$$

    a. It has infinite numbers of solutions
    b. 0 and 1
    c. It has no solutions
    d. 0

7. Turn the following expression into a simple polynomial:

$5(3x^2 - 2) - x^2(2 - 3x)$

    a. $3x^3 + 17x^2 - 10$
    b. $3x^3 + 13x^2 + 10$
    c. $-3x^3 - 13x^2 - 10$
    d. $3x^3 + 13x^2 - 10$

8. Solve $(x^3 + 2)(x^2 - x) - x^5$.

    a. $2x^5 - x^4 + 2x^2 - 2x$
    b. $-x^4 + 2x^2 - 2x$
    c. $-x^4 - 2x^2 - 2x$
    d. $-x^4 + 2x^2 + 2x$

9. $9ab^2 + 8ab^2 =$

    a. ab^2
    b. $17ab^2$
    c. 17
    d. $17a^2b^2$

10. Factor the polynomial $x^2 - 7x - 30$.

    a. $(x + 15)(x - 2)$
    b. $(x + 10)(x - 3)$
    c. $(x - 10)(x + 3)$
    d. $(x - 15)(x + 2)$

11. If a and b are real numbers, solve the following equation: $(a + 2)x - b = -2 + (a + b)x$

    a. -1
    b. 0
    c. 1
    d. 2

12. If $A = -2x^4 + x^2 - 3x$, $B = x^4 - x^3 + 5$ **and** $C = x^4 + 2x^3 + 4x + 5$, **find A + B - C.**

    a. $x^3 + x^2 + x + 10$
    b. $-3x^3 + x^2 - 7x + 10$
    c. $-2x^4 - 3x^3 + x^2 - 7x$
    d. $-3x^4 + x^3 + x^2 - 7x$

13. $(4Y^3 - 2Y^2) + (7Y^2 + 3y - y) =$

    a. $4y^3 + 9y^2 + 4y$
    b. $5y^3 + 5y^2 + 3y$
    c. $4y^3 + 7y^2 + 2y$
    d. $4y^3 + 5y^2 + 2y$

14. Turn the following expression into a simple polynomial: $1 - x(1 - x(1 - x))$

a. $x^3 + x^2 - x + 1$
b. $-x^3 - x^2 + x + 1$
c. $-x^3 + x^2 - x + 1$
d. $x^3 + x^2 - x - 1$

15. $7(2y + 8) + 1 - 4(y + 5) =$

a. $10y + 36$
b. $10y + 77$
c. $18y + 37$
d. $10y + 37$

16. Richard gives 's' amount of salary to each of his 'n' employees weekly. If he has 'x' amount of money then how many days he can employ these 'n' employees.

a. sx/7n
b. 7x/nx
c. nx/7s
d. 7x/ns

17. Factor the polynomial $x^2 - 3x - 4$.

a. $(x + 1)(x - 4)$
b. $(x - 1)(x + 4)$
c. $(x - 1)(x - 4)$
d. $(x + 1)(x + 4)$

18. Solve the inequality: $(2x + 1)/(2x - 1) < 1$.

a. $(-2, +\infty)$
b. $(1, +\infty)$
c. $(-\infty, -2)$
d. $(-\infty, 1/2)$

19. Using the quadratic formula, solve the quadratic equation:

$(a^2 - b^2)x^2 + 2ax + 1 = 0$

a. $a/(a + b)$ and $b/(a + b)$
b. $1/(a + b)$ and $a/(a + b)$
c. $a/(a + b)$ and $a/(a - b)$
d. $-1/(a + b)$ and $-1/(a - b)$

20. Turn the following expression into a simple polynomial: $(a + b)(x + y) + (a - b)(x - y) - (ax + by)$

a. $ax + by$
b. $ax - by$
c. $ax^2 + by^2$
d. $ax^2 - by^2$

21. Given polynomials $A = 4x^5 - 2x^2 + 3x - 2$ **and** $B = -3x^4 - 5x^2 - 4x + 5$, **find** $A + B$.

a. $x^5 - 3x^2 - x - 3$
b. $4x^5 - 3x^4 + 7x^2 + x + 3$
c. $4x^5 - 3x^4 - 7x^2 - x + 3$
d. $4x^5 - 3x^4 - 7x^2 - x - 7$

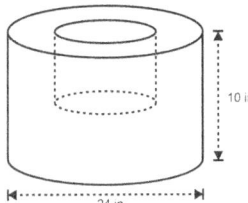

Note: figure not drawn to scale

22. What is the volume of the above solid made by a hollow cylinder that is half the size (in all dimensions) of the larger cylinder?

    a. 1440 π in³
    b. 1260 π in³
    c. 1040 π in³
    d. 960 π in³

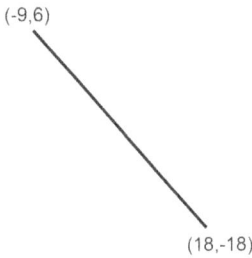

23. What is the slope of the line above?

    a. -8/9
    b. 9/8
    c. -9/8
    d. 8/9

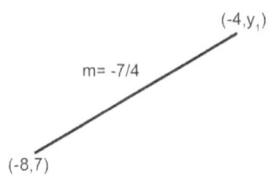

24. With the data given above, what is the value of y_1?

a. 0
b. -7
c. 7
d. 8

25. The area of a rectangle is 20 cm². If one side increases by 1 cm and other by 2 cm, the area of the new rectangle is 35 cm². Find the sides of the original rectangle.

a. (4,8)
b. (4,5)
c. (2.5,8)
d. b and c

26. What is the distance between the two points?

a. ≈19
b. 22
c. ≈21
d. ≈20

27. Find the solution for the following linear equation:
1/(4x - 2) = 5/6

   a. 0.2
   b. 0.4
   c. 0.6
   d. 0.8

28. How much water can be stored in a cylindrical container 5 meters in diameter and 12 meters high?

   Note: figure not drawn to scale

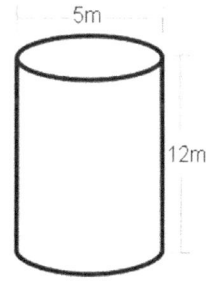

   a. 235.65 m³
   b. 223.65 m³
   c. 240.65 m³
   d. 252.65 m³

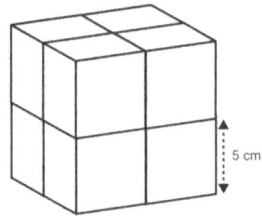

5 cm

Note: figure not drawn to scale

29. Assuming the figure above is composed of cubes, what is the volume?

    a. 125 cm³
    b. 875 cm³
    c. 1000 cm³
    d. 500 cm³

30. Solve

$x\sqrt{5} - y = \sqrt{5}$
$x - y\sqrt{5} = 5$

    a. $(0, -\sqrt{5})$
    b. $(0, \sqrt{5})$
    c. $(-\sqrt{5}, 0)$
    d. $(\sqrt{5}, 0)$

Writing

Directions: Choose the word or phrase that best completes the sentence.

1. _____ won first place in the Western Division?

    a. Whom
    b. Which
    c. What
    d. Who

2. There are now several ways to listen to music, including radio, CDs, and Mp3 files _____ you can download onto an MP3 player.

    a. on which
    b. who
    c. whom
    d. which

3. As the tallest monument in the United States, the St. Louis Arch _____ to an impressive 630 feet.

    a. has rose
    b. is risen
    c. rises
    d. No change is necessary.

4. The tired, old woman should _____ on the sofa.

    a. lie
    b. lays
    c. laid
    d. None of the options are correct.

5. Did the students understand that Thanksgiving always _____ on the fourth Thursday in November?

   a None of the options are correct.

   b. falling

   c. has fell

   d. falls

6. Collecting stamps, _____ models, and listening to shortwave radio were Rick's main hobbies.

   a. building

   b. build

   c. having built

   d. None of the options are correct.

7. Every morning, after the kids _____ for school and before the sun came up, my mother makes herself a cup of cocoa.

   a. had left

   b. leave

   c. have left

   d. None of the options are correct.

8. Elaine promised to bring the camera _____ at the mall yesterday.

   a. by me

   b. with me

   c. at me

   d. to me

9. Last night, he _____ the sleeping bag down beside my mattress.

    a. lay
    b. lain
    c. has laid
    d. laid

10. I would have bought the shirt for you if _____ you liked it.

    a. had known
    b. have known
    c. would know
    d. None of the options are correct.

11. Until you _____ the overdue books to the library, you can't take any new ones home.

    a. take
    b. bring
    c. None of the choices are correct.

12. If they had gone to the party, he would _____ too.

    a. gone
    b. went
    c. have went
    d. had went

13. His doctor suggested that he eat _____ snacks and do less lounging on the couch.

    a. less

    b. fewer

    c. None of the choices are correct.

14. His father is _____.

    a. a poet and novelist

    b. a poet and a novelist

    c. either of the above

    d. none of the above

15. Choose the sentence with the correct punctuation.

    a. George wrecked John's car that was the end of their friendship.

    b. George wrecked John's car. that was the end of their friendship.

    c. The sentence is correct.

    d. None of the choices are correct.

16. Choose the sentence with the correct punctuation.

    a. The dress was not Gina's favorite; however, she wore it to the dance.

    b. None of the choices are correct.

    c. The dress was not Gina's favorite, however; she wore it to the dance.

    d. The dress was not Gina's favorite however, she wore it to the dance.

17. Choose the sentence with the correct punctuation.

a. Chris showed his dedication to golf in many ways, for example, he watched all of the tournaments on television.

b. The sentence is correct.

c. Chris showed his dedication to golf in many ways, for example; he watched all of the tournaments on television.

d. Chris showed his dedication to golf in many ways for example he watched all of the tournaments on television.

18. Choose the sentence with the correct grammar.

a. If Joe had told me the truth, I wouldn't have been so angry.
b. If Joe would have told me the truth, I wouldn't have been so angry.
c. I wouldn't have been so angry if Joe would have told the truth.
d. If Joe would have telled me the truth, I wouldn't have been so angry.

19. Choose the sentence with the correct punctuation.

a. I can never remember how to use those two common words, "sell," meaning to trade a product for money, or sale- meaning an event where products are traded for less money than usual.

b. I can never remember how to use those two common words, "sell," meaning to trade a product for money, or "sale," meaning an event where products are traded for less money than usual.

c. I can never remember how to use those two common words, "sell," meaning to trade a product for money, or sale, meaning an event where products are traded for less money than usual.

d. None of the above are correct.

20. Choose the sentence with the correct punctuation.

a. The class just finished reading, -"Leinengen versus the Ants," a short story by Carl Stephenson about a plantation owner's battle with army ants.

b. The class just finished reading, Leinengen versus the Ants, a short story by Carl Stephenson about a plantation owner's battle with army ants.

c. The class just finished reading, "Leinengen versus the Ants," a short story by Carl Stephenson about a plantation owner's battle with army ants.

d. None of the above

21. Choose the sentence with the correct punctuation.

a. My best friend said, "always count your change."

b. My best friend said, "<u>Always Count your Change</u>."

c. My best friend said, "Always count your change."

d. None of the choices are correct.

22. Choose the sentence that is written correctly.

a. He told him to rise it up

b. He told him to raise it up

c. Either of the above

d. None of the above

23. Choose the sentence that is written correctly.

a. I shall arrive early and I will have breakfast with you

b. I shall arrive early and I would have breakfast with you

c. I shall arrive early and have breakfast with you.

d. None of the above

24. Choose the sentence that is written correctly.

a. The gold coins with the diamonds is to be seized
b. The gold coins with the diamonds are to be seized.
c. None of the above

25. Choose the sentence that is written correctly.

a The trousers are to be delivered today
b. The trousers is to be delivered today.
c. Both of the above

26. Choose the sentence that is written correctly.

a. She was nodding her head, her hips are swaying.
b. She was nodding her head, her hips is swaying.
c. She was nodding her head, her hips were swaying.
d. None of the above

27. Choose the sentence that is written correctly.

a. The sad news were delivered this morning
b. The sad news are delivered this morning.
c. The sad news was delivered this morning
d. None of the above

28. Choose the sentence that is written correctly.

a. The sentence is correct
b. Mathematics are my best subject in school
c. Mathematics was my best subject in school
d. Mathematics were my best subject in school.

29. Choose the sentence that is written correctly.

a. 15 minutes is all the time you have to complete the test.

b. 15 minutes are all the time you have to complete the test.

c. Both of the above.

d. None of the above.

30. Choose the sentence that is written correctly.

a. Everyone are to wear a black tie.

b. Everyone have to wear a black tie.

c. Everyone has to wear a black tie.

d. None of the above.

Answer Key

Reading Comprehension

1. A
Choice B is incorrect; the author did not express their opinion on the subject matter. Choice C is incorrect, the author was not trying to prove a point, nor is the author trying to persuade.

2. C
Choice C is correct; historians believe it was brutal and bloody. Choice A is incorrect; there is no consensus that the Crusades achieved great things. Choice B is incorrect; it did not stabilize the Holy Lands. Choice D is incorrect, some historians do believe this was the purpose but not all historians.

3. D
The feudal system led to infighting. Choice A is incorrect, it had the opposite effect. Choice B is incorrect, though this is a good answer, it is not the best answer. The Church asked for volunteers not the Feudal Lords. Choice C is incorrect, it did have an effect on the Crusades.

4. A
Saracen was a generic term for Muslims widely used in Europe during the later medieval era.

5. B
This warranty does not cover a product that you have tried to fix yourself. From paragraph two, "This limited warranty does not cover ... any unauthorized disassembly, repair, or modification. "

6. C
ABC Electric could either replace or repair the fan, provided the other conditions are met. ABC Electric has the option to repair or replace.

7. B
The warranty does not cover a stove damaged in a flood. From the passage, "This limited warranty does not cover any damage to the product from improper installation, accident, abuse, misuse, natural disaster, insufficient or excessive electrical supply, abnormal mechanical or environmental conditions."

A flood is an "abnormal environmental condition," and a natural disaster, so it is not covered.

8. A
A missing part is an example of defective workmanship. This is an error made in the manufacturing process. A defective part is not considered workmanship.

9. D
This question tests the reader's summarization skills. The other choices A, B, and C focus on portions of the second paragraph that are too narrow and do not relate to the specific portion of text in question. The complexity of the sentence may mislead students into selecting one of these answers, but rearranging or restating the sentence will lead the reader to the correct answer. In addition, choice A makes an assumption that may or may not be true about the intentions of the company, choice B focuses on one product rather than the idea of the products, and choice C makes an assumption about women that may or may not be true and is not supported by the text.

10. B
This question tests reader's attention to detail. If a reader selects A, he or she may have picked up on the use of the word "debate" and assumed, very logically, that the two are at odds because they are fighting; however, this is simply not supported in the text. Choice C also uses very specific quotes from the text, but it rearranges and gives them false meaning. The artists want to elevate their creations above the creations of other artists, thereby showing that they are "creative" and "innovative." Similarly, choice D takes phrases straight from the text and rearranges and confuses them. The artists are described as wanting to be "creative, innovative, individual people," not the women.

11. A

This question tests reader's vocabulary and summarization skills. This phrase, used by the author, may seem flippant and dismissive if readers focus on the word "whatever" and misinterpret it as a popular, colloquial term. In this way, choices B and C may mislead the reader to selecting one of them by including the terms "unimportant" and "stupid," respectively. Choice D is a similar misreading, but doesn't make sense when the phrase is at the beginning of the passage and the entire passage is on media messages. Choice A is literarily and contextually appropriate, and the reader can understand that the author would like to keep the introduction focused on the topic the passage is going to discuss.

12. A

This question tests a reader's inference skills. The extreme use of the word "all" in choice B suggests that every single advertising company are working to be approachable, and while this is not only unlikely, the text specifically states that "more" companies have done this, signifying that they have not all participated, even if it's a possibility that they may some day. The use of the limiting word "only" in choice C lends that answer similar problems; women are still buying from companies who do not care about this message, or those companies would not be in business, and the passage specifies that "many" women are worried about media messages, but not all. Readers may find choice D logical, especially if they are looking to make an inference, and while this may be a possibility, the passage does not suggest or discuss this happening. Choice A is correct based on specifically because of the relation between "still working" in the answer and "will hopefully" and the extensive discussion on companies struggles, which come only with progress, in the text.

13. C

This question tests the reader's summarization skills. The entire passage is leading up to the idea that the president of the US may not have had grounds to assert his Fourteen Points when other countries had lost so much. Choice A is pretty directly inferred by the text, but it does not adequately summarize what the entire passage is trying to communicate. Choice B may also be inferred by the passage when it says that the war is "imminent," but it does not represent the entire message, either. The passage does seem to be in praise of FDR, or at least in respect of him, but it does not in any way claim that he is the smartest president, nor does this represent the many other points included. Choice C is then the obvious answer, and most directly relates to the closing sentences which it rewords.

14. C
This question tests the reader's attention to detail. The passage does state that choices A and B are true, and while those statements are in proximity to the explanation for why the war started, they are not the reason given. Choice D is a mix up of words used in the passage, which says that the largest powers were in play but not that this fact somehow started the war. The passage does make a direct statement that a domino effect started the war, supporting choice C as the correct answer.

15. A
This question tests the reader's understanding of functions in writing. Throughout the passage, it states that leaders of other nations were hesitant to accept generous or peaceful terms because of the grievances of the war, and the great loss of life was chief among these. While the passage does touch on the devastation of deadly weapons (B), the use of this raw, emotional fact serves a much larger purpose, and the focus of the passage is not the weapons. While readers may indeed consider who lost the most soldiers (C) when, so many countries were involved and the inequalities of loss are mentioned in the passage, there is no discussion of this in the passage. Choice D is related to A, but choice A is more direct and relates more to the passage.

16. B
This question tests the reader's vocabulary skills. Choice A may seem appealing to readers because it is phonetically similar to "catalyzed," but the two are not related in any other way. Choice C makes sense in context, but if plugged in to the sentence creates a redundancy that doesn't make sense. Choice D does also not make sense contextually, even if the reader may consider that funds were needed to create more weaponry, especially if it was advanced.

17. A
Victoria is about 5 miles from Burnaby.

18. B
The Village Hall is about 5 miles from Victoria.

19. A
The correct order of ingredients is brown sugar, baking soda and chocolate chips.

20. B
Sturdy: strong, solid in structure or person. In context, Stir in chocolate chips by hand with a *sturdy* wooden spoon.

21. A
Disperse: to scatter in different directions or break up. In context, Stir until the chocolate chips and nuts are evenly *dispersed*.

22. B
You can stop stirring the nuts when they are evenly distributed. From the passage, "Stir until the chocolate chips and nuts are evenly dispersed."

23. B
Choice A is incorrect as the Monster killed Frankenstein, not the other way around. Choice B is correct, Frankenstein is dead. Choice C is incorrect - Mary Shelley is the author. Choice D is incorrect, the person is called Frankenstein.

24. C
The speaker 'suspended' from following through on his duty to destroy the monster due to curiosity and compassion. The other choices may seem reasonable, but are not explicitly given in the passage.

25. D
All the choices are correct. Frankenstein's monster destroys Frankenstein by

    a. By killing Frankenstein

    b. By letting himself be the monster everyone sees him as

    c. By destroying everything Frankenstein loved

26. A

Superfluous means unnecessary. Looking at the context of the word as it is used in the passage:

"Your repentance," I said, "is now superfluous. If you had listened to the voice of conscience and heeded the stings of remorse before you had urged your diabolical vengeance to this extremity, Frankenstein would yet have lived."

27. B

The time limit for radar detectors is 14 days. Since you made the purchase 15 days ago, you do not qualify for the guarantee.

28. B

Since you made the purchase 10 days ago, you are covered by the guarantee. Since it is an advertised price at a different store, ABC Electric will "beat" the price by 10% of the difference, which is,

500 – 400 = 100 – difference in price

100 X 10% = $10 – 10% of the difference

The advertised lower price is $400. ABC will beat this price by 10% so they will refund $100 + 10 = $110.

29. C

The purpose of this passage is to persuade.

30. B

The correct answer can be found in the fourth sentence of the first paragraph.

Choice A is incorrect because repenting begins the day AFTER Mardi Gras. Choice C is incorrect because you can celebrate Mardi Gras without being a member of a Krewe.

Choice D is incorrect because exploration does not play any role in a modern Mardi Gras celebration.

MATHEMATICS

1. D
Area of Type B consists of two rectangles and a half circle. We can find these three areas and sum them up in order to find the total area:

Area of the left rectangle: $(4 + 8) * 8 = 96$ m^2

Area of the right rectangle: $14 * 8 = 112$ m^2

The diameter of the circle is equal to 14 m. So, the radius is $14/2 = 7$:

Area of the half circle = $(1/2) * \pi r^2 = (1/2) * (22/7) * (7)^2 = (1 * 22 * 49)/(2 * 7) = 77$ m^2

Area of Type B = $96 + 112 + 77 = 285$ m^2

Converting this area to ft^2: 285 m^2 = $285 * 10.76$ ft^2 = 3066.6 ft^2

Type B is (3066.6 - 1300 = 1766.6 ft^2) 1766.6 ft^2 larger than type A.

2. B
To solve the equation, we need the equation in the form $ax2 + bx + c = 0$.

$0.9x^2 + 1.8x - 2.7 = 0$ is already in this form.

The quadratic formula to find the roots of a quadratic equation is:

$x_{1,2} = (-b \pm \sqrt{\Delta}) / 2a$ where $\Delta = b^2 - 4ac$ and is called the discriminant of the quadratic equation.

In our question, the equation is $0.9x^2 + 1.8x - 2.7 = 0$. To eliminate the decimals, let us multiply the equation by 10:

$9x^2 + 18x - 27 = 0$ ... This equation can be simplified by 9 since each term contains 9:

$x^2 + 2x - 3 = 0$

By remembering the form $ax^2 + bx + c = 0$:

$a = 1$, $b = 2$, $c = -3$

So, we can find the discriminant first, and then the roots of the equation:

$\Delta = b^2 - 4ac = (2)^2 - 4 * 1 * (-3) = 4 + 12 = 16$

$x_{1,2} = (-b \pm \sqrt{\Delta}) / 2a = (-2 \pm \sqrt{16}) / 2 = (-2 \pm 4) / 2$

This means that the roots are,

$x_1 = (-2 - 4)/2 = -3$ and $x_2 = (-2 + 4)/2 = 1$

4. C

First, we need to arrange the two equations to obtain the form $ax + by = c$. We see that there are 3 and 2 in the denominators of both equations. If we equate all at 6, then we can cancel all 6 in the denominators and have straight equations:

Equate all denominators at 6:

$2(4x + 5y)/6 = 3(x - 3y)/6 + 4 * 6/6$ ... Now we can cancel 6 in the denominators:

$8x + 10y = 3x - 9y + 24$ ... We can collect x and y terms on left side of the equation:

$8x + 10y - 3x + 9y = 24$

$5x + 19y = 24$ ... Equation (I)

Let us arrange the second equation:

$3(3x + y)/6 = 2(2x + 7y)/6 - 1 * 6/6$ ... Now we can cancel 6 in the denominators:

$9x + 3y = 4x + 14y - 6$ ... We can collect x and y terms on left side of the equation:

$9x + 3y - 4x - 14y = -6$

5x - 11y = -6 ... Equation (II)

Now, we have two equations and two unknowns x and y. By writing the two equations one under the other and operating, we can find one unknowns first, and find the other next:

   5x + 19y = 24

-1/ 5x - 11y = -6 ... If we substitute this equation from the upper one, 5x cancels -5x:

   5x + 19y = 24

   -5x + 11y = 6 ... Summing side-by-side:

   5x - 5x + 19y + 11y = 24 + 6

   30y = 30 ... Dividing both sides by 30:

   y = 1

Inserting y = 1 into either of the equations, we can find the value of x. Choosing equation I:

5x + 19 * 1 = 24

5x = 24 - 19

5x = 5 ... Dividing both sides by 5:

x = 1

So, x = 1 and y = 1 is the solution; it is shown as (1, 1).

5. A
x^2 + 12x - 13 = 0 ... We try to separate the middle term 12x to find common factors with x^2 and -13 separately:

x^2 + 13x - x - 13 = 0 ... Here, we see that x is a common factor for x^2 and 13x, and -1 is a common factor for -x and -13:

x(x + 13) - 1(x + 13) = 0 ... Here, we have x times x + 13 and -1 times x + 13 summed up. This means that we have x - 1 times x + 13:

(x - 1)(x + 13) = 0

This is true when either or, both of the expressions in the parenthesis are equal to zero:

x - 1 = 0 ... x = 1

x + 13 = 0 ... x = -13

1 and -13 are the solutions for this quadratic equation.

6. C
This equation has no solution.

$x^2 + 4x + 4 + x^2 - 4x + 4 / (x - 2)(x + 2) = 0$

$2x^2 + 8 / (x - 2)(x + 2) = 0 \Rightarrow 2x^2 + 8 = 0$
$x^2 + 4 = 0$
$x_{1,2} = 0 \pm \sqrt{-4 * 4} / 2$
$x_{1,2} = 0 \pm \sqrt{-16} / 2$
Solution for the square root of -16 is not a real number, so this equation has no solution.

7. D
We need to distribute the factors to the terms inside the related parenthesis:

$5(3x^2 - 2) - x^2(2 - 3x) = 15x^2 - 10 - (2x^2 - 3x^3)$

$= 15x^2 - 10 - 2x^2 + 3x^3$

$= 3x^3 + 15x^2 - 2x^2 - 10$ ... similar terms written together to ease summing/substituting.

$= 3x^3 + 13x^2 - 10$

8. B
We need to distribute the factors to the terms inside the related parenthesis:

$(x^3 + 2)(x^2 - x) - x^5 = x^5 - x^4 + (2x^2 - 2x) - x^5$

$= x^5 - x^4 + 2x^2 - 2x - x^5$

$= x^5 - x^5 - x^4 + 2x^2 - 2x$ ... similar terms written together to ease summing/substituting.

$= -x^4 + 2x^2 - 2x$

9. B

To simplify the expression, we need to find common factors. We see that both terms contain the term ab^2. So, we can take this term out of each term as a factor:

$ab^2 (9 + 8) = 17ab^2$

10. C

$x^2 - 7x - 30 = 0$ ... We try to separate the middle term $-7x$ to find common factors with x^2 and -30 separately:

$x^2 - 10x + 3x - 30 = 0$ ... Here, we see that x is a common factor for x^2 and $-10x$, and 3 is a common factor for $3x$ and -30:

$x(x - 10) + 3(x - 10) = 0$ ... Here, we have x times $x - 10$ and 3 times $x - 10$ summed up. This means that we have $x + 3$ times $x - 10$:

$(x + 3)(x - 10) = 0$ or $(x - 10)(x + 3) = 0$

11. A

We need to simplify the equation by distributing factors and then collecting x terms on one side, and the others on the other side:

$(a + 2)x - b = -2 + (a + b)x$

$ax + 2x - b = -2 + ax + bx$

$ax + 2x - ax - bx = -2 + b$ ... ax and -ax cancel each other:

$2x - bx = -2 + b$ ... we take -1 as a factor on the right side:

$(2 - b)x = -(2 - b)$

$x = -(2 - b)/(2 - b)$ ... Simplifying by $2 - b$:

$x = -1$

12. C

We are asked to find A + B - C. By paying attention to the sign distribution; we write the polynomials and operate:

$A + B - C = (-2x^4 + x^2 - 3x) + (x^4 - x^3 + 5) - (x^4 + 2x^3 + 4x + 5)$

$= -2x^4 + x^2 - 3x + x^4 - x^3 + 5 - x^4 - 2x^3 - 4x - 5$

$= -2x^4 + x^4 - x^4 - x^3 - 2x^3 + x^2 - 3x - 4x + 5 - 5$ ... similar terms written together to ease summing/substituting.

$= -2x^4 - 3x^3 + x^2 - 7x$

13. D
To simplify, we remove parenthesis:

$(4y^3 - 2y^2) + (7y^2 + 3y - y) = 4y^3 - 2y^2 + 7y^2 + 3y - y$ ... Then, we operate within similar terms:

$= 4y^3 + (-2 + 7)y^2 + (3 - 1)y = 4y^3 + 5y^2 + 2y$

14. C
To obtain a polynomial, we should remove the parenthesis by distributing the related factors to the terms inside the parenthesis:
$1 - x(1 - x(1 - x)) = 1 - x(1 - (x - x * x)) = 1 - x(1 - x + x^2)$

$= 1 - (x - x * x + x * x^2) = 1 - x + x^2 - x^3$ ... Writing this result in descending order of powers:

$= -x^3 + x^2 - x + 1$

15. D
To simplify the expression, remove the parenthesis by distributing the related factors to the terms inside the parenthesis:

$7(2y + 8) + 1 - 4(y + 5) = (7 * 2y + 7 * 8) + 1 - (4 * y + 4 * 5)$

$= 14y + 56 + 1 - 4y - 20$

$= 14y - 4y + 56 + 1 - 20$ ... similar terms written together to ease summing/substituting.

$= 10y + 37$

16. D
We understand that each of the n employees earn s amount of salary weekly. This means that one employee earns s salary weekly. So; Richard has ns amount of money to employ n employees for a week.

We are asked to find the number of days n employees can be employed with x amount of money. We can do simple direct proportion:

If Richard can employ n employees for 7 days with ns amount of money,

Richard can employ n employees for y days with x amount of money ... y is the number of days we need to find.

We can do cross multiplication:

y = (x * 7)/(ns)

y = 7x/ns

17. A
x^2 - 3x - 4 ... We try to separate the middle term -3x to find common factors with x^2 and -4 separately:

x^2 + x - 4x - 4 ... Here, we see that x is a common factor for x^2 and x, and -4 is a common factor for -4x and -4:

= x(x + 1) - 4(x + 1) ... Here, we have x times x + 1 and -4 times x + 1 summed up. This means that we have x - 4 times x + 1:

= (x - 4)(x + 1) or (x + 1)(x - 4)

18. D
We need to simplify and have x alone and on one side in order to solve the inequality:

(2x + 1)/(2x - 1) < 1

(2x + 1)/(2x - 1) - 1 < 0 ... We need to write the left side at the common denominator 2x - 1:

(2x + 1)/(2x - 1) - (2x - 1)/(2x - 1) < 0

(2x + 1 - 2x + 1)/(2x - 1) < 0 ... 2x and -2x terms cancel each other in the numerator:

2/(2x - 1) < 0

2 is a positive number; so,

2x - 1 < 0

$2x < 1$

$x < 1/2$ ... This means that x should be smaller than $1/2$ and not equal to $1/2$. This is shown as $(-\infty, 1/2)$.

19. D

To solve the equation, we need the equation in the form $ax^2 + bx + c = 0$.

$(a^2 - b^2)x^2 + 2ax + 1 = 0$ is already in this form.

The quadratic formula to find the roots of a quadratic equation is:

$x_{1,2} = (-b \pm \sqrt{\Delta}) / 2a$ where $\Delta = b^2 - 4ac$ and is called the discriminant of the quadratic equation.

In our question, the equation is $(a^2 - b^2)x^2 + 2ax + 1 = 0$.

By remembering the form $ax^2 + bx + c = 0$: $a = a^2 - b^2$, $b = 2a$, $c = 1$

So, we can find the discriminant first, and then the roots of the equation:

$\Delta = b^2 - 4ac = (2a)^2 - 4(a^2 - b^2) * 1 = 4a^2 - 4a^2 + 4b^2 = 4b^2$

$x_{1,2} = (-b \pm \sqrt{\Delta}) / 2a = (-2a \pm \sqrt{4b^2}) / (2(a^2 - b^2)) = (-2a \pm 2b) / (2(a^2 - b^2))$

$= 2(-a \pm b) / (2(a^2 - b^2))$ ... We can simplify by 2:

$= (-a \pm b) / (a^2 - b^2)$

This means that the roots are,

$x_1 = (-a - b) / (a^2 - b^2)$ ... $a^2 - b^2$ is two square differences:

$x_1 = -(a + b) / ((a - b)(a + b))$ ... $(a + b)$ terms cancel each other:

$x_1 = -1/(a - b)$

$x_2 = (-a + b) / (a^2 - b^2)$ ... $a^2 - b^2$ is two square differences:

$x_2 = -(a - b) / ((a - b)(a + b))$ ... $(a - b)$ terms cancel each other:

$x_2 = -1/(a + b)$

20. A
To simplify, we need to remove the parenthesis and see if any terms cancel:

$(a + b)(x + y) + (a - b)(x - y) - (ax + by) = ax + ay + bx + by + ax - ay - bx + by - ax - by$

By writing similar terms together:

$= ax + ax - ax + bx - bx + ay - ay + by + by - by$ ... + terms cancel - terms:

$= ax + by$

21. C
We are asked to add polynomials A + B. By paying attention to the sign distribution; we write the polynomials and operate:

$A + B = (4x^5 - 2x^2 + 3x - 2) + (-3x^4 - 5x^2 - 4x + 5)$

$= 4x^5 - 2x^2 + 3x - 2 - 3x^4 - 5x^2 - 4x + 5$ ... Writing similar terms together:

$= 4x^5 - 3x^4 - 2x^2 - 5x^2 + 3x - 4x - 2 + 5$ ... Operating within similar terms:

$= 4x^5 - 3x^4 - 7x^2 - x + 3$

22. B
Total Volume = Volume of large cylinder - Volume of small cylinder

Volume of a cylinder = area of base * height = $\pi r^2 * h$

Total Volume = $(\pi * 12^2 * 10) - (\pi * 6^2 * 5) = 1440\pi - 180\pi$

$= 1260\pi \text{ in}^3$

23. A

Slope (m) = $\dfrac{\text{change in y}}{\text{change in x}}$

If we know the coordinates of two points on a line, we can find the slope (m) with the below formula:

$m = (y_2 - y_1)/(x_2 - x_1)$ where (x_1, y_1) represent the coordinates of one point and (x_2, y_2) the other.

In this question:

$(-9, 6) : x_1 = -9, y_1 = 6$

$(18, -18) : x_2 = 18, y_2 = -18$

Inserting these values into the formula:

$m = (-18 - 6)/(18 - (-9)) = (-24)/(27)$ ... Simplifying by 3:

$m = -8/9$

24. A

If we know the coordinates of two points on a line, we can find the slope (m) with the below formula:
$m = (y_2 - y_1)/(x_2 - x_1)$ where (x_1, y_1) represent the coordinates of one point and (x_2, y_2) the other.

In this question:

$(-4, y_1) : x_1 = -4, y_1 =$ we will find

$(-8, 7) : x_2 = -8, y_2 = 7$

$m = -7/4$

Inserting these values into the formula:

$-7/4 = (7 - y_1)/(-8 - (-4))$

$-7/4 = (7 - y_1)/(-8 + 4)$

$7/(-4) = (7 - y_1)/(-4)$ ... Simplifying the denominators of both sides by -4:

$7 = 7 - y_1$

$0 = -y_1$

$y_1 = 0$

25. D

The area of a rectangle is found by multiplying the width to the length. If we call these sides with "a" and "b"; the area is = a * b.

We are given that a * b = 20 cm² ... Equation I

One side is increased by 1 and the other by 2 cm. So new side lengths are "a + 1" and "b + 2".

The new area is (a + 1)(b + 2) = 35 cm² ... Equation II

Using equations I and II, we can find a and b:

ab = 20

(a + 1)(b + 2) = 35 ... We need to distribute the terms in parenthesis:

ab + 2a + b + 2 = 35

We can insert ab = 20 to the above equation:

20 + 2a + b + 2 = 35

2a + b = 35 - 2 - 20

2a + b = 13 ... This is one equation with two unknowns. We need to use another information to have two equations with two unknowns which leads us to the solution. We know that ab = 20. So, we can use a = 20/b:

2(20/b) + b = 13

40/b + b = 13 ... We equate all denominators to "b" and eliminate it:

40 + b² = 13b

b² - 13b + 40 = 0 ... We can use the roots by factoring. We

try to separate the middle term -13b to find common factors with b^2 and 40 separately:

$b^2 - 8b - 5b + 40 = 0$ ⋯ Here, we see that b is a common factor for b^2 and -8b, and -5 is a common factor for -5b and 40:

$b(b - 8) - 5(b - 8) = 0$ Here, we have b times b - 8 and -5 times b - 8 summed up. This means that we have b - 5 times b - 8:

$(b - 5)(b - 8) = 0$

This is true when either or both of the expressions in the parenthesis are equal to zero:

b - 5 = 0 ... b = 5

b - 8 = 0 ... b = 8

So we have two values for b which means we have two values for a as well. In order to find a, we can use any equation we have. Let us use a = 20/b.

If b = 5, a = 20/b → a = 4

If b = 8, a = 20/b → a = 2.5

So, (a, b) pairs for the sides of the original rectangle are: (4, 5) and (2.5, 8). These are found in (b) and (c) answer choices.

26. D

The distance between two points is found by = $[(x_2 - x_1)^2 + (y_2 - y_1)^2]^{1/2}$

In this question:

(18, 12) : $x_1 = 18$, $y_1 = 12$

(9, -6) : $x_2 = 9$, $y_2 = -6$

Distance= $[(9 - 18)^2 + (-6 - 12)^2]^{1/2}$

= $[(-9)^2 + (-18)^2]^{1/2}$

$= (9^2 + 2^2 * 9^2)^{1/2}$

$= (9^2(1 + 5))^{1/2}$ ... We can take 9 out of the square root:

$= 9 * 6^{1/2}$

$= 9\sqrt{6}$

$= 9 * 2.45$

$= 22.04$

The distance is approximately 22 units.

27. D
$1/(4x - 2) = 5/6$ ... We can do cross multiplication:
$5(4x - 2) = 1 * 6$ ... Now, we distribute 5 to the parenthesis:

$20x - 10 = 6$ ... We need x term alone on one side:

$20x = 6 + 10$

$20x = 16$ ... Dividing both sides by 20:

$x = 16/20$ ... Simplifying by 2 and having 10 in the denominator provides us finding the decimal equivalent of x:

$x = 8/10 = 0.8$

28. A
The formula of the volume of cylinder is the base area multiplied by the height. As the formula:

Volume of a cylinder = $πr^2h$. Where π is 3.142, r is radius of the cross sectional area, and h is the height.

We know that the diameter is 5 meters, so the radius is 5/2 = 2.5 meters.

The volume is: V = $3.142 * 2.5^2 * 12 = 235.65$ m³.

29. C
The large cube is made up of 8 smaller cubes with 5 cm sides. The volume of a cube is found by the third power of

the length of one side.
Volume of the large cube = Volume of the small cube * 8

$= (5^3) * 8 = 125 * 8$

$= 1000$ cm³

There is another solution for this question. Find the side length of the large cube. There are two cubes rows with 5 cm length for each. So, one side of the large cube is 10 cm.

The volume of this large cube is equal to $10^3 = 1000$ cm³

30. A
First write the two equations one under the other. Our aim is to multiply equations with appropriate factors to eliminate one unknown and find the other, and then find the eliminated one using the found value.

$-\sqrt{5}/$ $x\sqrt{5} - y = \sqrt{5}$ ... If we multiply this equation by $\sqrt{5}$, y terms will cancel each other:

$\quad x - y\sqrt{5} = 5$

$-x\sqrt{5}\sqrt{5} + y\sqrt{5} = -\sqrt{5}\sqrt{5}$ ... using $\sqrt{5}\sqrt{5} = 5$:

$\quad x - y\sqrt{5} = 5$

$\quad -5x + y\sqrt{5} = -5$

$\quad x - y\sqrt{5} = 5$ ... Summing side-by-side:

$\quad -5x + y\sqrt{5} + x - y\sqrt{5} = -5 + 5$ ... $+ y\sqrt{5}$ and $- y\sqrt{5}$, -5 and $+ 5$ cancel each other:

$\quad -4x = 0$

$\quad x = 0$

Now, using either of the equations gives us the value of y. Let us choose equation 1:

$x\sqrt{5} - y = \sqrt{5}$

$0\sqrt{5} - y = \sqrt{5}$

$-y = \sqrt{5}$

$y = -\sqrt{5}$

The solution to the system is $(0, -\sqrt{5})$

WRITING

1. D
"Who" is correct because the question uses an active construction. "To whom was first place given?" is passive construction.

2. D
"Which" is correct, because the files are objects and not people.

3. C
The simple present tense, "rises," is correct.

4. A
"Lie" does not require a direct object, while "lay" does. The old woman might lie on the couch, which has no direct object, or she might lay the book down, which has the direct object, "the book."

5. D
The simple present tense, "falls," is correct because it is repeated action.

6. A
The present progressive, "building models," is correct in this sentence; it is required to match the other present progressive verbs.

7. C
Past Perfect tense describes a completed action in the past, before another action in the past.

8. D
The preposition "to" is the correct preposition to use with "bring."

9. D
"Laid" is the past tense.

10. A
This is a past unreal conditional sentence. It requires an 'if' clause and a result clause, and either clause can appear first. The 'if' clause uses the past perfect, while the result clause uses the past participle.

11. C
Bring vs. Take. Usage depends on your location. Something coming your way is brought to you. Something going away is taken from you.

12. A
The sentence is correct. Went vs. Gone. Went is the simple past tense. Gone is used in the past perfect.

13. B
Fewer vs. Less. 'Fewer' is used with countables and 'less' is used with uncountables.

14. B
His father is a poet and a novelist. It is necessary to use 'a' twice in this sentence for the two distinct things.

15. C
The semicolon links independent clauses. An independent clause can form a complete sentence by itself.

16. A
The semicolon links independent clauses with a conjunction (However).

17. B
The sentence is correct. The semicolon links independent clauses. An independent clause can form a complete sentence by itself.

18. A
The third conditional is used for talking about an unreal situation (that did not happen) in the past. For example, "If I had studied harder, [if clause] I would have passed the

exam [main clause]. Which is the same as, "I failed the exam, because I didn't study hard enough."

19. B
Here the word "sale" is used as a "word" and not as a word in the sentence, so quotation marks are used.

20. C
Titles of short stories are enclosed in quotation marks, and commas always go inside quotation marks.

21. A
Quoted speech is not capitalized.

22. B
The verb raise ('to increase', 'to lift up.') can appear in three forms, raise, raised and raised.

23. C
The two verbs "shall" and "will" should not be used in the same sentence when referring to the same future.

24. B
When two subjects are linked with "with" or "as well," use the verb form that matches the first subject.

25. A
Use a plural verb for nouns like measles, tongs, trousers, riches, scissors etc.

26. C
A verb can fit any of the two subjects in a compound sentence since the verb form agrees with that subject.

27. C
Always use the singular verb form for nouns like politics, wages, mathematics, innings, news, advice, summons, furniture, information, poetry, machinery, vacation, scenery etc.

28. C
Always use the singular verb form for nouns like politics, wages, mathematics, innings, news, advice, summons, furniture, information, poetry, machinery, vacation, scenery etc.

29. A
Use a singular verb with a plural noun that refers to a specific amount or quantity that is considered as a whole (dozen, hundred score etc).

30. C
Use a singular verb with either, each, neither, everyone and many.

Conclusion

CONGRATULATIONS! You have made it this far because you have applied yourself diligently to practicing for the exam and no doubt improved your potential score considerably! Getting into a good school is a huge step in a journey that might be challenging at times but will be many times more rewarding and fulfilling. That is why being prepared is so important.

Good Luck!

Register for Free Updates and More Practice Test Questions

Register your purchase at www.test-preparation.ca/register.html for fast and convenient access to updates, errata, free test tips and more practice test questions.

www.ingramcontent.com/pod-product-compliance
Lightning Source LLC
Chambersburg PA
CBHW070915080526
44589CB00013B/1311